byron bay

A taste of the region

Nelly le Comte Remy Tancred

take a seat, relax and enjoy

warm nights glittering days

Welcome

Coffee at one of the local cafes was our first destination. Between us we had years of experience in the publishing industry and strong connections to the Northern NSW community, to restaurants, farmers and market stall holders. We shared a passion for delicious food, stunning imagery and high quality publishing. Byron Bay seemed like a fruitful place to throw around an idea; to publish a book that would showcase the quality and diversity of cuisine being grown, produced and cooked in the region – a book full of beautiful, lush images and accessible recipes that would showcase local eateries and provide a culinary map of the area for visitors, tourists and locals.

Our concept? To document our journey around the region; from Yamba in the south to Kingscliff in the north, and then west to Nimbin collecting the recipes of producers, caterers and restaurateurs along the way and capturing images of their food. Byron Bay, a taste of the region, is the result.

We are very proud of this sumptuous book, which contains recipes from all over Northern NSW and creates a whole new 'foodies' map of the region.

With the overwhelming success of our first edition selling out, it was time we revised the book; Byron Bay a taste of the region.

Since the first edition of the book in 2013, our region has seen many new restaurants and cafes open. Our enriched edition features many of these as well as new recipes from some featured in the first edition and several favourites remain published again in this edition.

This enriched edition, contains recipes from all over Northern NSW and creates a `foodies' map of the region. Long known as a tourist mecca and sea-changer destination, this picturesque semi-tropical area is a fertile food bowl, renowned for the quality of its produce and the ingenuity of its growers and producers. Byron Bay sits uniquely at the centre of this beautiful land, so for us it seemed like a good place to start.

We're inviting you to take the journey with us as we follow three distinct routes: commencing in Byron we venture south, over the hills to the west, and following the sun we finally head north. Along the way we meet dozens of incredibly creative foodies, and each trip offers you a rich and tantalizing array of recipes straight from the kitchens of the best chefs and producers of the region. Flip through the yummy pages of this beautiful book, testament to the love of what we do, and the wonderful culmination of what ended up being an awesome tasting tour!

We hope you enjoy the flavours as much as we did. Next time you're in town, visit a restaurant in the book. They are a friendly bunch and your taste buds will thank you!

Romy and Nelly

MACLEAN
YAMBA
ILUKA
EVANS HEAD
BYRON BAY
CORAL SEA

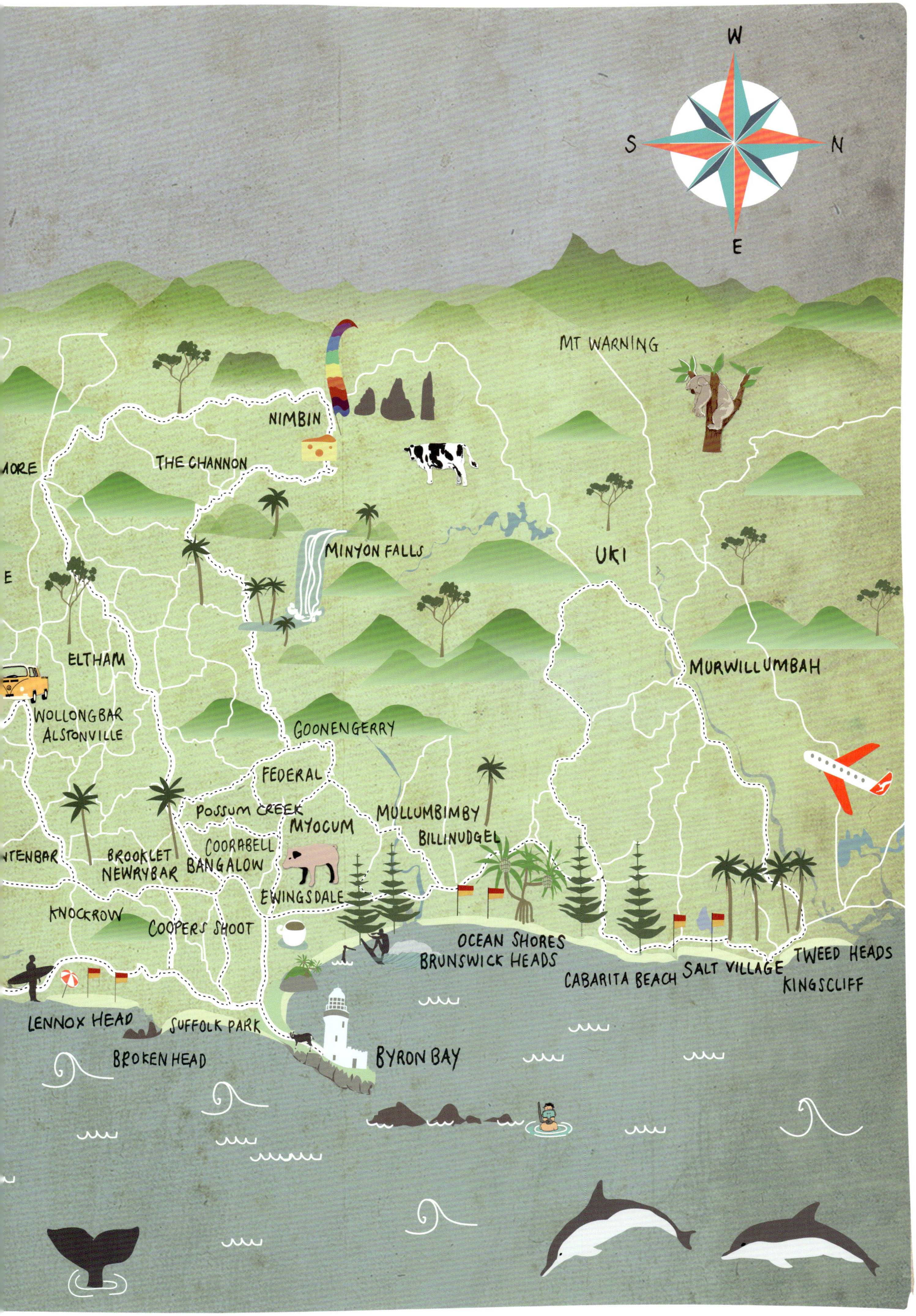
W
S
N
E
MT WARNING
NIMBIN
MORE
THE CHANNON
MINYON FALLS
UKI
E
ELTHAM
MURWILLUMBAH
WOLLONGBAR
ALSTONVILLE
GOONENGERRY
FEDERAL
POSSUM CREEK
MYOCUM
MULLUMBIMBY
BILLINUDGEL
COORABELL
BANGALOW
NTENBAR
BROOKLET
NEWRYBAR
EWINGSDALE
KNOCKROW
COOPERS SHOOT
OCEAN SHORES
BRUNSWICK HEADS
CABARITA BEACH
SALT VILLAGE
TWEED HEADS
KINGSCLIFF
LENNOX HEAD
SUFFOLK PARK
BROKEN HEAD
BYRON BAY

places to cast a line or pack
your board and surf the point

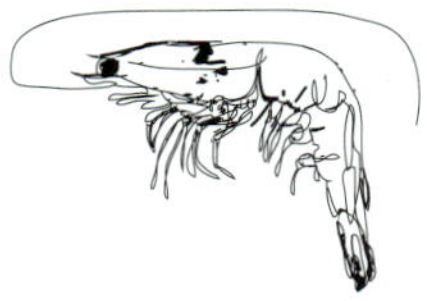

South bound

The southern section of our region is less populated, but no less interesting or productive. This journey tracks the lazy old Richmond River from Ballina. For the most part you will travel across floodplains: perfectly flat and largely treeless, prolific with sugar cane; these lime green expanses are hypnotically beautiful.

Consistently providing a beautiful backdrop to a road trip you are welcomed to the cute hinterland towns of Tintenbar, Newrybar and Alstonville, plus those sleepy river sugar towns of Maclean and Woodburn.

For the most part, the journey takes you along the coast to visit some of the most idyllic seaside villages that Australia has to offer: through Lennox Head, Ballina and finally to Yamba, where it is surely time for a seafood cocktail.

Monique Guterres

Lemon Miso Scallops

with green pawpaw and ogo nori pickle

SERVES 20 AS A CANAPE

20 scallops in half shell

Ogo nori pickle

small green pawpaw, julienned
1 tbs chopped ogo nori*
¼ cup Japanese rice wine vinegar
¼ cup water
2 tbs raw sugar

Miso sauce

1 knob of ginger
2 tbs shiro miso (white miso)
1 lemon fine zested + strained juice
1 tsp honey
1 tbs extra virgin olive oil
small daikon finely julienned
small handful red and green micro shiso
2 tbs toasted sesame seeds

Pat scallops dry. Marinate in half of the miso sauce for minimum 1 hour.

For miso sauce, finely grate ginger and lemon zest, then add the honey and lemon juice, whisk in olive oil.

In a saucepan simmer vinegar, water and sugar for 10 mins.

With scissors chop ogo nori into short strands and add to pawpaw.

Mix the dailkon, shiso and sesame together.

Fry scallops until just cooked through.

Put a tablespoon of ogo nori pickle on centre of each scallop shell, lay scallop on each nest.

Spoon left over sauce onto each scallop.

Top each scallop with shiso mix.

*Ogo Nori - wild harvested red Australian seaweed.

Hungry Like The Wolf

Antipasti Plank

SERVES 4

Brussels sprouts, fresh peas and green olives

2 cloves garlic
250g Brussels sprouts, chopped in half
100g podded fresh peas
80g green olives
sea salt

Battered marinated white anchovies and sage

20 individual white anchovies
20 sage leaves
5 tbs plain flour
sparkling water
sea salt
cracked black pepper
vegetable oil for deep frying

Maple syrup and lemon thyme baked ricotta

200g fresh ricotta
1 fried egg
2 tbs maple syrup
few sprigs lemon thyme
sea salt
cracked black pepper
olive oil

For the Brussels sprouts, heat oil and fry garlic to golden and add the Brussels sprouts with a couple of tablespoons of water and fry until golden.

Add the olives followed by the peas, sauté and keep warm.

For the battered marinated white anchovies, drain the anchovies from the oil on absorbent paper.

Press the anchovy and the inside leaf of sage together.

Prepare batter by adding water to flour until a thick pancake consistency.

Dredge anchovy and sage in batter and deep-fry until golden.

Drain on absorbent paper and season with salt and pepper.

For the baked ricotta, mash ricotta and egg with maple syrup and lemon thyme leaves.

Line an oven-proof mould with baking paper and spoon in ricotta.

Bake for 15 minutes in preheated 170°C oven.

Remove from mould and invert on to baking tray.

Drizzle with oil, maple syrup, salt and pepper and return to oven until a light brown colour.

Serve warm in bowls on plank together with char-grilled sourdough bread.

Byron Bay Pork Shoulder

from the Byron at Byron

SERVES 8

2kg boneless pork shoulder (rind on)
2 small brown onions
2 organic garlic bulbs, halved
2 fennel bulbs, sliced
1 leek, cut in half
6 heirloom carrots (yellow, purple, traditional orange)
thyme
rosemary
knob of butter
salt and pepper
macadamia oil
your favourite well loved earthenware casserole dish

Preheat oven to 160°C.

Ask your local butcher to cut you a nice piece of pork shoulder. Cut the vegetables neatly into large pieces. Place in an oven-proof dish and place the pork on top. The secret to a good crackling is to make sure that the pork skin is dry and well scored. You can use a very sharp kitchen knife for this. Massage macadamia oil and sea salt into the pork skin and place in a preheated oven at 160°C for around 3 to 3½ hours. Meat juices should be clear when tested, although using a meat thermometer is the best guide, aiming at approximately 70°C . When meat is cooked internally, turn the oven up to high and start to blister the skin (crackling). Alternatively, place under the hot grill section of your oven, being careful not to burn the skin.

Rinse the carrots (don't peel them) then place in separate small pans, not mixing the colours, and adding enough water to cover. Place a small knob of butter in each pan together with salt and a sprig of thyme then cook until soft and glazed. Keep in a warm place.

To serve, place pork in its roasting dish surrounded by a tricolour of carrots. Slice through the crunchy crackling and serve with roasting gravy, a leafy market garden salad and apple sauce.

Byron Bay Pork Bali Curry

with sprouting salad green papaya and radishes

SERVES 8

Curry paste
10 cloves garlic
4 shallots, peeled
100g chillies, de-seeded
200g fresh ginger
100g galangal
2 lemongrass stalks
6 kaffir lime leaves
6 coriander roots
1 tsp coriander seeds, lightly roasted
1 tsp cumin seeds, lightly roasted
1 star anise
1 cinnamon quill
100g roasted macadamia nuts
1 cup papaya, finely sliced
3 tbs shredded coconut, toasted
1 tsp shrimp paste
2kg Byron Bay pork scotch, chopped into bite-size pieces
3 – 4 tbs macadamia oil

Sauce
100g palm sugar
2 tbs ketjap manis
2 tbs fish sauce
500ml coconut cream
100ml tamarind purée
approx 1ltr chicken stock
lime juice to taste

To make the curry paste, pound all ingredients together in mortar and pestle into a fine paste. Note: paste freezes well in small containers.

Using a thick heavy-based pan, fry the paste in macadamia oil for 10–15 minutes, stirring all the time, until fragrant. Allow to cool.

Add more macadamia oil to the pan and fry the pork in batches, making sure the meat is nicely browned.

Add approximately 500g of the cooked curry paste to the browned pork, then add the sauce ingredients. Simmer gently until meat is cooked, approximately 90 minutes.

When cooked, adjust the seasoning to balance the flavours so that the dish is sweet, sour and salty. The flavours should not dominate and the balance should be pleasant.

Serve with steamed rice, greens, sprouts, radishes, green papaya, crispy onions and macadamia nuts.

The Park Hotel's Pan-Roasted Baby Lamb Rump

with rosemary-scented crushed kipfler potatoes, confit asparagus and eschalot soubise

SERVES 6

6 baby lamb rumps, 'cap' or fatty layer left on
2 bunches asparagus
¼ bunch rosemary
1kg kipfler potatoes
1 tbs dried oregano
100g unsalted butter
2 cloves garlic, crushed

Soubise

200g peeled eschalots
1 pinch nutmeg
100ml pouring cream

Slice eschalots finely and place in a medium saucepan with 50 gram butter. Leave on as low heat as possible for 45 minutes, stirring occasionally (try not to colour).

While eschalots are cooking, scrub Kipfler potatoes till quite clean, cover with cold water add a pinch of salt and simmer till cooked. Place on a tray and cool in refrigerator. Add pouring cream to the now well-stewed eschalots and reduce by half.

Puree with stick blender, add nutmeg and season to taste. Once potatoes are cool, crush them with your hands to pieces no bigger than a 5 cent coin. Heat a large fry pan and cook crushed potatoes, dried oregano, chopped rosemary, garlic and remaining butter. Sauté till lightly coloured then season to taste.

Score the 'cap' of the lamb rumps and place cap-side down in a pan on a low heat. Render for 5 minutes then place rumps in the oven and cook at 180°C for 9 minutes. Place asparagus around the lamb in the juices and rest the lamb for 5 minutes – the juices will cook the asparagus.

Slice lamb and serve on top of potatoes with asparagus and soubise.

Fast Ed's

Spinach and Egg Meatloaf

SERVES 4

4 slices white bread, crusts removed
400g English spinach leaves, stems removed
400g beef mince
400g pork mince
1 cup pecorino, finely grated
¼ bunch rosemary leaves, chopped
1 tsp ground nutmeg
2 eggs, beaten
1 brown onion, finely diced
2 cloves garlic, minced
salt flakes and freshly-milled black pepper
4 hard-boiled eggs, peeled
¼ cup extra virgin olive oil
250ml beef stock
150ml dry white wine

Preheat the oven to 210°C. Place the bread in a food processor and pulse until fine crumbs form. Blanch the spinach leaves in boiling water until just wilted, then refresh in iced water. Squeeze out the excess moisture, chop finely then set aside.

Combine the breadcrumbs with the minces, cheese, rosemary, nutmeg, beaten eggs, onion and garlic in a large bowl and mix well.

Season with salt and pepper.

Spread half the mixture on a lined oven tray in a 10cm x 20cm rectangle. Top with half the spinach and arrange the boiled eggs on top. Place the remaining spinach on the eggs and the remaining mince mixture on top. Form into a domed log shape.

Brush the log with oil and bake for 15 minutes. Pour the stock and wine over and continue baking for another 30 minutes, basting often. Cool, then slice and serve.

The Balcony's

Paella 'Valencia'

SERVES 2

100 ml olive oil
1 medium onion
1 medium red capsicum
4 garlic cloves
1 medium red chilli
1/2g saffron
200g calasparra or bomba rice
50g spinach
2 medium tomatoes (seeded and diced)
1 tsp parsley
100g boneless chicken thigh
4 large prawns
100g calamari
100g chorizo
8 large mussels
50g peas
800ml chicken stock
1 tsp paprika
1 tsp salt

In a flat ovenproof pan, gently warm olive oil. Add onions, garlic, chilli and capsicum cook slowly for 3 minutes. Turn up heat and add chicken and chorizo. Cook for another 3 minutes. Add rice, saffron, paprika and salt. Gently stir together. Add stock and calamari, mix and simmer for 5 minutes without stirring.

Arrange and push prawns and mussels into the rice. Turn heat down to low and cook for 14 minutes. Turn the pan every 2 minutes on low, to ensure even cooking. Turn heat off. Cover with tea towel for 5 minutes.

Just before serving add garnish of spinach, peas and diced tomato.

NOTE: We always use Paella style rice such as "Bomba or Calasparra" for authenticity and best results.

Paella is pronounced Pah-eh-yah

Italian at the Pacific

Carpaccio

SERVES 4-6

Pastrami spice

27g coriander seeds (toasted)
36g cumin seeds (toasted)
18g white peppercorns (toasted)
9g cayenne pepper
30g sweet paprika

Salt cure

300g coarse salt
100g sugar
bunch of thyme
bunch of rosemary
zest of 1 lemon
1 lemongrass stick
5g star anise
2 cinnamon sticks
5g cardamom pods
5g black pepper
5g fennel seeds
5g coriander seeds

Fish

1 side of kingfish (pin-boned and skin off)

Dressing

juice of 1 lemon
100ml olive oil

Garnish

1 head of fennel (shaved finely, remove root)
2 oranges (segments, cut into three)
toasted almonds (whole, cut into three after toasting)
2 bunches celery heart (just leaves)
4 baby radishes (thinly sliced)
microherbs

For pastrami spice, grind up whole ingredients with cayenne pepper and paprika and set aside.

For salt mix, toast all spices, chop herbs and place all ingredients in blender until herbs and spices are coarsely broken down.

For the fish, place half the salt mixture in the bottom of a large metal tray. Lay kingfish on top and then cover with the remaining salt mixture. Leave in the fridge over-night (10-12 hours). Remove from salt, rinse well and dry with a clean tea towel. Cut the kingfish into three equal pieces. Dust heavily on all sides with the pastrami spice. Place into a very hot pan (without oil) for ten seconds on each side and return immediately to the fridge.

To prepare the dressing, add the juice of one lemon to the olive oil, whisk well.

To serve, thinly slice the kingfish and arrange onto plates (roughly 10-12 slices per serve). Garnish with shaved fennel, orange segments, toasted almonds, celery heart, microherbs and drizzle with lemon dressing.

Important note: do not add any extra salt as the fish is already cured.

Slow Cooked Lamb Shoulder for Two

The Beach Hotel

SERVES 2

1.2kg lamb forequarter, centre bone cut out
1 sprig rosemary
1 brown onion
1 large carrot
4 cloves garlic
200ml beef stock
salt/pepper
100g pumpkin, diced
100g sweet potato, diced
100g chat potatoes, halved
6 baby turnips
2 medium beetroots, diced
olive oil, salt, pepper

Yoghurt sauce
300ml natural yoghurt
½ lemon juiced
1 tsp salt
1 tbs ground cumin

Preheat oven to 110°C. Chop onion, carrot and garlic in halves. Place in ovenproof dish with beef stock and rosemary. Place seasoned lamb on top and wrap with foil. Cook for 5 hours or until tender on middle shelf of oven. Once cooked remove from oven and allow to cool. Strain off liquid and place on low heat and simmer. Reduce to sauce consistency.

Turn oven up to 180°C. Place chopped vegetables in oven proof dish. Drizzle with olive oil, salt and pepper. Bake in oven for 30 minutes or until cooked through and golden. While vegetables are cooking, combine ingredients for yoghurt sauce and prepare. Once lamb has cooled enough to handle, season skin with a good amount of salt. Heat oil in a pan; once hot, place lamb skin side down for 3-5 minutes until skin is golden and crispy.

To serve: Place lamb in middle of platter and drizzle with pan sauce. Add vegetables and a side of yoghurt sauce. Shred, share and enjoy!

Quattro's

Saffron Brodetto: Fisherman's Stew

SERVES 2-3

50g butter
2 tbs diced shallots
4 cloves garlic, thinly sliced
150ml dry white wine
10 strands saffron
250ml cream
2 x 400g tins whole peeled tomatoes
handful basil, roughly torn
salt and pepper
1 large Moreton Bay or Balmain bug (approx 400g), halved and cleaned
8 mussels
6 large local king prawns, peeled and deveined
6 scallops
200g fresh local fish (mahi mahi and jewfish here)
150ml dry white wine
1 washed leek, 1cm thick sliced on the angle
ciabatta
whole garlic cloves
olive oil
flat leaf parsley

Melt the butter in a medium pot, then add garlic and shallots. Sauté until the garlic is fragrant, about 1 minute. Add the saffron and stir well, then add the wine and simmer for 5 minutes or until reduced by half. Add cream and reduce. Now add the tomatoes and simmer for 10 minutes then throw in torn basil and simmer for another 3 minutes, season to taste. Allow to cool a little, then blitz until smooth. Force through fine sieve and set aside.

Heat 1 tablespoon olive oil in a large heavy bottom fry pan, add halved bugs flesh side down and cook on medium heat for 3 minutes, turn over. Increase heat and add fish, prawns and scallops, sauté on high for 1-2 minutes, turning to sear on all sides. Add wine and mussels together then the leeks, as mussels start to open. Add a generous amount of saffron /tomato sauce then simmer on low until all fish is cooked.

Drizzle extra virgin olive oil onto ciabatta and toast and rub with garlic cloves then dress with finely chopped parsley and sea salt.

Season with coarse sea salt and freshly cracked black pepper and serve in a pan or portion into dishes, garnished with plenty of coarsely chopped flat leaf parsley and fresh lemon. Top with garlic ciabatta.

Beef and Beach Kobe Wagyu Fillet with Mushroom Crust, Pomme Fondant

and a watercress salad and Roquefort and peppercorn sauce

SERVES 6

6 x 180g Kobe beef fillets (or any other high quality beef fillet

Pomme fondant

6 large desiree potatoes, peeled
1½ ltrs chicken stock
150g butter
pinch of salt

Roquefort sauce

1 cup thickened cream
100g Roquefort
1½ tbs green peppercorns
fine zest of 1 lemon

Crisp salad

200g sugar snap peas, trimmed of spine
1 bunch red radishes, thinly sliced
3 punnets baby watercress, trimmed

Salad dressing

2 tbs lemon juice
½ tsp Dijon mustard
salt and pepper
100ml extra virgin olive oil

Gourmet mushroom crust

1 clove garlic, crushed
150g eschalot, finely diced
60ml olive oil
150g mixed mushrooms (shitake, enoki, oyster, shimiji, button, swiss browns)
¼ cup panko breadcrumbs
30g melted butter
30g grated parmesan
30g grated tasty cheese
salt and pepper to taste

For pomme fondant, cut the top and bottom off each potato and using a pastry cutter cut out the middle to form a cylinder. Spread soft butter 1cm thick in a heavy-based saucepan, push potatoes into the butter, season evenly with the salt and just cover potatoes with chicken stock. Place on high heat and boil until the stock is almost reduced and potatoes are soft. Lower heat to medium/low and gently simmer until the butter has browned and caramelised and all liquid reduced. Cool then remove.

For the Roquefort sauce, heat cream, lemon zest and peppercorns and simmer for 2 minutes.

Lower the heat, add the cheese and stir to combine, blending until smooth. Season to taste.

Place salad dressing ingredients in jar and shake vigorously until emulsified.

For mushroom crust, gently sauté eschalots and garlic in oil until soft. Increase heat to high and quickly add mushrooms. Stir frequently until mushrooms are browned and cooked.

Transfer to a bowl, cool slightly and mix with remaining ingredients. Season and set aside.

Season the beef fillets then sear in a hot pan, sealing first side for 3-4 minutes or until brown crust has formed. Turn over once only and seal 3 minutes, remove from pan and allow to rest on tea towel for 5 minutes. Top with mushroom crust mix.

To serve, mix salad ingredients together in bowl. Have sauce warm on the stove.

Place the pomme fondant and warm steaks topped with mushroom crust on a shallow baking tray and cook in heated 220°C oven for 3-5 minutes or until crust is brown and pomme fondant is hot. Remove steaks from tray and rest on tea towel again for 1 minute.

Place pomme fondant on plate, spoon on sauce to form a pond, place steak in pond and finish with salad.

Foam's

Prawns with Pickled Wombok and Miso Caramel

SERVES 4 - ENTRÉE SIZE

Pickled wombok

half a wombok cabbage
5 cloves garlic
1 tbs salt
30ml fish sauce
50g ginger
1 tsp sugar
1/4 cup korean chilli paste (kimchi)

Miso caramel

100g sugar
water
1 tbs miso

Puffed black rice

2 cups of canola oil
2 tablespoons black rice
red shiso for garnish

To make black rice, place oil in pan, bring up to 195°C heat, pour black rice into the oil and cook for approx 20 seconds. Rice will puff up,strain oil into a non-melting container, and place puffed rice on a tray with paper towel.

To make the pickled wombok, cut cabbage into 1 inch squares, sprinkle with salt, place in a colander with a bowl underneath and leave in the fridge for 24 hours. Rinse cabbage and squeeze out excess water, slice garlic and ginger thinly, mix with chilli paste, sugar, cabbage and fish sauce, leave for 2-3 days for flavours to intensify.

To make the miso caramel, place sugar and ¼ cup hot water in a pan, bring to boil and turn down to a moderate heat, Cook to 170°C; (if using a sugar thermometer, the caramel will start colouring at 160°C) when caramel has reached 170°C add ¼ cup of water (please use caution when adding water to caramel, the caramel is very hot and will react violently) add the miso paste, the caramel will harden in places, cook on low heat until the hard pieces of caramel re-dissolve. Transfer to a container for later use.

To prepare prawns, do not shell the prawns but cut them through the back of the head and down theback to the tail but not all the way through (butterfly), clean out the intestinal tract.

Drizzle prawns with canola oil and season with sea salt, grill prawns cut side down on a very hot char or grill for 30 seconds then turn over and cook for around another 30 seconds until the prawns are cooked and the shells have colour to plate.

Position grilled prawns on plate, place pickled cabbage over prawns (around two tablespoons) and drizzle caramel miso over top.

Garnish with red shiso and puffed black rice.

This recipe will make more than the required portions, but as it tastes so good, it will get used quickly.

The Point Ballina

Chilli King Prawn and Basil Linguine

SERVES 2

200g cooked medium king prawns
200g linguine or pasta of your choice
salt
½ bunch fresh basil leaves

Roasted items

2 roasted red chillies
½ punnet cherry tomatoes

Tomato sauce

200g ripe tomatoes
50g garlic
pinch of dry chilli flakes
20ml extra virgin olive oil
pinch of salt

Toss the cherry tomatoes and chillies with a little olive oil and salt and roast for 12 minutes at 220°C.

Prepare the tomato sauce by roughly chopping garlic and tomatoes. Sweat garlic in a pan with the olive oil and chilli flakes until just starting to brown. Add the chopped tomatoes and cook on low temperature for approximately 20 minutes. Add a squeeze of lemon and salt to taste. If the sauce becomes too thick add a touch of water.

Cook the pasta in salted boiling water until just cooked then strain, ready to put in your sauce.

Peel and devein king prawns then cook in a pan with a little olive oil, salt and fresh basil leaves.

To serve, heat up tcmato sauce, add prawn mixture and cooked pasta and add seasoning. Top with roasted cherry tomatoes and whole roasted chillies.

The Point Ballina

Oven Baked Snapper and Surf Clams in whole roasted garlic cream

SERVES 2

1 fresh baby snapper, or any fresh firm white fish
100g surf clams
200ml cream
50ml white wine
40g brown onion
60g fresh garlic
100ml olive oil
2 pieces of organic sourdough
200g potatoes (desiree or sebago)
5ml lemon juice
1 celery stick
1 bay leaf
sea salt to taste
pinch of paprika
whole roasted garlic confit

Peel a whole garlic bulb (approximately 50 grams) and place in a small oven-proof dish, cover with olive oil and roast at 160°C for approx 20 minutes or until the garlic is soft.

To prepare the fish, make sure fish is cleaned and scaled and ready to go. Score on both sides, drizzle with olive oil (or garlic confit oil) and salt generously. Bake in 200°C oven for 15–20 minutes.

Cut the potatoes into wedges and drizzle with a little olive oil, or use some of the garlic oil from the confit. Add sea salt and paprika and roast in a hot oven at 200°C for 15–20 minutes.

Note: be sure not to cut the potatoes too thick or they may take longer to cook through. These can go in the oven at the same time as your fish.

To make the cream sauce and surf clams, in a little oil sweat off the onions, garlic and celery, taking care not to brown. Add white wine and reduce by half then add bay leaf, surf clams or mussels, lemon juice and a pinch of salt and simmer on a low heat, reducing until it coats the back of a spoon. Remove celery stalk and bay leaf and add herbs of your choice to serve.

Note: if you reduce your sauce too much, just add a touch of water to correct it.

Serve with lemon and warm sourdough.

The Boardwalk's

Steamed Mussels with Tomato, Chorizo, Garlic, Lemon and Parsley

SERVES 4

1kg black mussels
2 cloves garlic thinly sliced
2 large ripe tomatoes chopped
6 cherry tomatoes cut in half
150ml white wine
100g Salumi chorizo sausage chopped
3 tbs chopped flatleaf parsley
1 lemon juice and zest
2 slices sourdough toasted

This is my favourite dinner any night of the week and a dish that is going to be on the new menu in the 'Boardwalk' this winter. It's so quick and easy and a good excuse to open a bottle of wine because you need to use some in the recipe.

Clean the mussels by taking all the beards of and scraping away any barnicles.

Heat a large pot and add some extra virgin olive oil with the sliced garlic and chorizo when the garlic starts to colour add the chopped tomatoes and cook for about a minute until they start to soften. Add the white wine and mussels and cover with a lid or some foil.

Shake the pan a few times and check after 1 minute to see if the mussels have opened.

If they have add ½ the chopped parsley and the juice of 1 lemon.

Lift the mussels and sauce into your dish and finish with the rest of the parsley and lemon zest.

Serve with sourdough or crusty bread and the rest of the chilled white wine.

Blake Seymour's

Balinese Prawn Curry

SERVES 6

500g peeled prawns

paste

6 cloves of garlic
2 red onions
10 red chilli
100g fresh tumeric
100g galangal
200g ginger
2 lemongrass stalks
6 kaffir lime leaves
roots of 1 bunch coriander
5g coriander seed
5g cumin seed

100ml vegetable oil
10g shrimp paste roasted
300g palm sugar
3 tbs fish sauce
100ml tamarind puree

100g macadamias roasted
1 ltr coconut cream
1 ltr water or stock

To make the paste, blend all raw vegetables in a food processor or mortar and pestle.

In a large heavy based saucepan cook paste on a low heat with the vegetable oil. This will usually take at least an hour and will go a darker red colour when completely cooked.

Once cooked add roasted shrimp paste, palm sugar, fish sauce and tamarind. Paste is now finished.

For the sauce, add 1 litre of fish stock, white chicken stock or water and reduce slightly. Blend the macadamias in the blender with 1 litre coconut cream and leaves of the coriander. Add to sauce. This will thicken the sauce while also giving it a real nutty creamy taste. Taste for seasoning might need salt, lime, palm sugar, tamarind, fish sauce or more blended chilli to balance.

When you are ready to serve add the prawns to the curry and briefly simmer to cook through.

Serve with steamed jasmine rice and sprout, radish and coriander salad.

Fleurs BBQ Balmain Bugs

with preserved lemon and chilli marinade

SERVES 4

8 Balmain bugs
lemon chilli marinade
100g preserved lemon (skin only)
2 large red chillies
60ml lime syrup
120ml extra virgin olive oil

Quinoa

2 cups quinoa
4 cups chicken stock
60g garlic cloves
1 bunch eschalots (white part only)
50ml extra virgin olive oil
¼ bunch chopped coriander

Pomegranate vinaigrette

1 pomegranate
1½ tbs vincotto
1 tbs truffle oil
1½ tbs pomegranate molasses
4 tbs lime syrup
6 tbs extra virgin olive oil

Halve the bugs and clean, trim legs and feelers (your local fishmonger can do this if preferred). Whisk lime syrup and olive oil. Finely dice preserved lemon skin and chilli (seeds removed) together, then add to the lime mixture.

Place quinoa and chicken stock in saucepan and bring to the boil. Cover and reduce heat to low and cook for 10 minutes. Turn off the heat and leave covered for a further 10 minutes. In a separate pan, fry in olive oil finely sliced whole garlic gloves and sliced eschalots until golden. Combine the quinoa and garlic mix with freshly chopped coriander.

Remove seeds and liquid from fresh pomegranate. Combine with vincotto, truffle oil, molasses, syrup and oil and whisk until combined.

Using a char-grill or BBQ on a medium to low heat, stand the bugs flesh-side up.

Baste the bug meat continuously during cooking with the preserved lemon marinade; they are cooked when the flesh turns from clear to white.

Serve the bugs on a bed of quinoa accompanied by the pomegranate dressing.

LAR

Sevtap's

Turkish-Style Sardines

SERVES 2

12 sardines, cleaned
3 tbs sunflower oil
2 vine-ripened tomatoes, diced
1 sm red onion, diced
2 handfuls flat-leaf parsley, chopped
125ml extra virgin olive oil
juice of 1 lemon
sea salt
lemon wedges, to serve

Wash the sardines and drain on paper towel. Heat the oil in a non-stick pan and cook the sardines for 2 minutes on each side over high heat, or until golden.

Place the tomato, onion, parsley, olive oil, lemon juice and salt in a large bowl and gently toss to combine. Divide the salad between 4 plates and arrange the sardines on top.

Serve with lemon wedges.

PACIFIC

VENTURA

YAMBA

Yamba Shores Tavern Mud Crab

in a sweet chilli sauce

SERVES 4

1kg mud crab, cleaned and quartered, claws cracked
2 tbs grated fresh ginger
1 lge fresh red chilli, diced and de-seeded if desired
2 tbs finely diced lemongrass
1 tbs finely diced garlic
4 fresh kaffir lime leaves, finely sliced
2 tbs coriander stalk, finely cut
3 tbs spanish onion, finely diced
vegetable oil
1 tsp sesame oil
500ml homemade tomato sauce
100ml tomato ketchup
100ml sweet chilli sauce
50ml sweet soy sauce
2 tbs caster sugar
2 shallots, finely sliced for garnish

Heat wok and add vegetable oil, then sesame oil, onion, ginger, lemongrass, garlic and chilli.

Add crab and toss, adding a little water to help the crab steam.

Add kaffir lime and coriander stalk followed by sweet chilli sauce, tomato sauce, ketchup and sweet soy sauce. Add sugar, turn down heat to a simmer then cook for 5–7 minutes.

Check seasoning and serve garnished with shallots.

Avocado with Parmesan and Cashew Crust

with Nicholson Fine Foods Beetroot Finishing Vinegar

SERVES 1

½ avocado, skin removed
15g salted cashew nuts, chopped
15g Parmigiano Reggiano (if possible; another brand is ok), finely grated
10g baby rocket leaves, washed and dried
1g Lightly Spiced Beetroot Seasoning Sprinkle (available from many quality food stores or directly from Nicholson Fine Foods)
25ml Euro Style Spiced Beetroot Finishing Vinegar (available from many quality food stores or directly from Nicholson Fine Foods)
10ml extra virgin olive oil

Select a large ripe avocado and cut in half. Carefully peel away the outer skin, leaving the inside intact.

Chop cashew nuts finely and mix with freshly grated parmesan. Sprinkle the nut/cheese mix on a plate and press the cut side of the avocado firmly into the mix. Turn over to check the surface is covered evenly and if not, repeat the process. With the avocado cut-side down, use a knife to slice a small flat surface at the top of the rounded side. This will help the avocado to sit nicely on the serving plate.

Gently turn the avocado over and position on the serving plate. Toss the rocket leaves in 10ml of the beetroot vinegar then pile into the hollow of the avocado. Sprinkle with the Lightly Spiced Beetroot Seasoning Sprinkle to finish the dish .

Serve with a cool crisp glass of white wine.

Belgian Chocolate Burger with Crushed Berries

Nicholson Fine Foods

SERVES 10

1 pkt Belgian Chocolate Mousse Classic Chocolate
150ml water
300ml thickened cream
1½ pkt biscuits (Chocolate Ripple)
fresh berries (strawberries, blueberries, raspberries), 1 punnet of each
50g caster sugar

Open the Belgian Chocolate mousse packet, measure water and stir in for 60 seconds. Whip cream until thick, fold in a fifth of it followed by the rest.

Spread biscuits on plastic-lined tray flat-side up.

Fill piping bag with mousse and pipe onto biscuits in a cone shape – the chocolate filling must be equal to the thickness of 2 biscuits when pressed down. Top mousse with second biscuit flat-side down and press lightly to level mousse to the outside edge of the biscuit. Cover with plastic wrap and store for minimum 12 hours to soften.

Wash, hull and halve strawberries. Warm blueberries in pan with half the sugar until they start to bleed. Remove from the heat and fold through the strawberries and remaining sugar and leave to cool. Fold in raspberries just prior to serving.

To serve, dust burgers with cocoa powder and serve with the crushed berries on one side and syrup drizzled around the plate. Burgers will keep for five days and may also be frozen for up to one month in a sealed container and served frozen on a hot day.

Clayton Donovan's

Macadamia Nut and Cheese Beignets with Native Reductions

SERVES 4 AS AN ENTREE

For the beignets

100ml water
25g butter
150g sifted plain flour
4g baking powder
65g coarsely ground Brookfarm macadamia nuts
3 egg yolks
2g finely chopped dill
2g finely chopped parsley
25g finely grated parmesan cheese
5g semolina
1g roasted ground fennel

Carrot and fennel reduction

200ml fresh carrot juice
½g fennel seeds
15g caster sugar

Balsamic and wattleseed reduction

200ml balsamic vinegar
1g wattleseed
50g caster sugar
50ml red wine
Davidson Plum Syrup
200ml fresh Davidson plum juice
1 tsp sesame oil
200ml sugar syrup
2g fresh ginger
¾ tsp xanthan gum

Apple foam

450ml apple juice
1 tbs lecithin

To make the beignets, heat water and remove from heat. Add the butter to melt it. Mix remaining beignets ingredients together until combined. Roll mix into small balls (dessertspoon-sized) and fry until lightly browned in hot oil. Finish off in the oven for 4–5 minutes at 150C.

Before plating up the beignets prepare the following:

To prepare the carrot reduction, put all the ingredients in a pan and bring to the boil , then simmer until thickened. Strain.

For balsamic/wattleseed reduction, put all the ingredients except wattleseed into a pan, bring to the boil and simmer until thickened. Remove from heat and add the wattleseed.

For Davidson Plum reduction, in a pan infuse the ginger in the sugar syrup with the sesame oil and bring to the boil. Strain into the Davidson plum juice, add xanthem gum, stir then strain the mixture again.

To make the apple foam, heat lecithin and apple juice together in saucepan until they reach blood temperature. Froth with hand-blender then pass through a fine sieve. Mix again with blender to create a foam without over-agitating mixture. Do not allow to cool.

Serve the beignets with roasted seasonal baby vegetables, topped with extra parmesan cheese, and dress the plate with the three reductions and the foam. Garnish with 10g LSA (linseed, sunflower and ground almond mix).

Summerland House Farm's

Baby Beetroot and Macadamia Salad

SERVES 2

125g cooked baby beetroot
125g cooked pumpkin, diced
¼ avocado, diced
60g mesclun leaves
30g baby spinach
50g feta, cubed
20g macadamia nuts, crushed
20ml balsamic dressing
rocket flowers to garnish

Cut baby beetroot in wedges and heat with the diced pumpkin in a moderately high oven 180°C .

Place the lettuce and spinach in the centre of large salad bowl and toss in diced avocado and feta.

Arrange warmed vegetables on top, dress with balsamic dressing and sprinkle with macadamia nuts and garnish with rocket flowers.

Summerland House Farm's

Orange and Macadamia Crusted Chicken Salad

SERVES 2

50g chicken tenderloins

Crumb mix

1½ cups bread crumbs
½ cup macadamia nuts crushed
1 tbs paprika
1½ tbs orange zest
2 eggs beaten
100ml orange juice
2 cups plain flour
salt and pepper

Dressing

1 cup mayonnaise
1 cup orange juice
zest of 1 orange
½ cup sour cream
1 tsp crushed ginger
¼ cup lime juice
¼ cup brown sugar

Salad

120g crumbed chicken
30g cucumber deseeded and sliced
¼ avocado sliced
4 cherry tomatoes halved
50g orange segments
10g baby spinach
20g mixed lettuce leaves
lemon balm leaves to garnish

Begin by mixing salt and pepper evenly through plain flour.

In a second bowl, combine eggs and orange juice to make an egg wash.

In another bowl place the bread crumbs with the orange zest, paprika and macadamias.

Dip chicken into flour then egg wash then crumbs to coat the chicken well. Deep fry in hot oil until golden.

Prepare dressing by blending all ingredients with a stick blender, adjusting the thickness by using more or less orange juice.

To make the salad, place leaves into salad bowl. Top with cherry tomatoes, cucumber, avocado and orange segments.

Placed cooked chicken pieces on top of the salad, dress with the citrus dressing and garnish with lemon balm leaves.

Sake-Infused Beef Cheek

with celeriac puree, pickled daikon and wasabi green salad

SERVES 4

Chicken stock

100g carrots
100g onions
100g celery
100g leek
1 chicken carcass
1 bay leaf
2 sprigs lemon thyme
2 black peppercorns
2½ ltr water

Beef cheeks

60ml sake
4 beef cheeks, 400g each
2 tbs tomato paste
2 tbs plain flour
1 tbs Dijon mustard
3 tbs grapeseed oil
20g palm sugar
1 cinnamon quill
2½ ltr chicken stock (cover)
1 lemon zest
20ml soy sauce
30g crispy eshalots
6 sprigs chives, finely sliced

Celeriac puree

100g butter
1 brown onion, sliced
½ celeriac (peeled, roughly chopped)
½ cauliflower (peeled, roughly chopped)
75ml pouring cream
250ml milk
2g sea salt
2g white pepper

Wasabi greens salad

1 bunch baby carrots, peeled
6 baby beetroot, peeled
10g wasabi greens
4 green shallots, chopped into batons

Soak beef in sake overnight to tenderise (at least 3-4 hours) then strain.

Bring chicken stock to the boil.

Rub flour, mustard and tomato paste on to meat. Heat 3 tablespoons of grapeseed oil in a casserole and seal meat both sides to colour (2 minutes each side). Add cinnamon quill and palm sugar to the stock then beef cheeks, ensuring they are fully covered. Bring to the boil then reduce to a low simmer and cook for 5-6 hours, or until soft. Skim pot regularly. Remove from sauce and reduce sauce until sticky, adding lemon zest and soy sauce to taste.

For celeriac puree, heat butter and sweat onions until translucent, about 4 minutes, then add cauliflower and celeriac. Pour in the milk and cream, season with salt and white pepper and cook for 15 minutes or until soft. Strain then blend until creamy in food processor.

For salad, boil baby carrots and beetroot, add 10g butter and season.

To serve, spoon puree onto plate, top with sliced beef cheeks and scatter over chives and crispy eshalots. Arrange pickled vegetables to one side of the plate, scatter on shallot batons and place wasabi greens and baby vegetables around the side.

For the Pickled Vegetables

500ml water
50ml mirin
1 tsp caster sugar
2 garlic bulbs
2 kaffir lime leaves
100ml rice wine vinegar
1 daikon, peeled and shaved lengthways
1 carrot, peeled and shaved lengthways
4 green shallots, sliced on angle
15g pickled ginger
50g bean sprouts
¼ bunch Vietnamese mint

For pickled vegetables, boil water, mirin, sugar, garlic, shallots, kaffir lime leaves and rice wine vinegar for 5 minutes. Add carrot, daikon, pickled ginger, Vietnamese mint and bean sprouts then remove from heat. Strain before serving.

Che Bon's Chocolate Parfait

with mandarin coulis

SERVES 6

110g good quality chocolate
2g agar agar
1/4 cup milk
3/4 cup cream
1/4 tsp coffee extract

Coulis

6 mandarins
1-2 cups sugar

Whisk cream into soft peaks. Soak the agar agar in water to cover.

Melt chocolate in double boiler. Bring the milk to the boil then add coffee extract and drained agar agar. Pour 1/3 of the milk on to the chocolate, whisking to incorporate, then slowly add another third, whisking in thoroughly, then finally whisk in the last third. When the mix has cooled a little add the cream. Place baking paper around the inside of 6 ring moulds. Pour the mousse into the rings and put in freezer for 2 hours.

For coulis, juice mandarins and strain. Place strained juice in a saucepan and slowly add the sugar, then reduce over low heat, stirring until sugar has dissolved. Taste for sweetness, adding more sugar if necessary, then place in fridge to cool half an hour before serving.

Remove baking paper and serve with mandarin coulis.

Quattro's

Classic Tiramisu Ascolana

SERVES 6

1kg good mascarpone (fat content higher than 50%, otherwise will not set)
6 eggs
2 tbs caster sugar
2 vanilla pods
1-2 packs savoiardi biscuits
6 double shots espresso
90ml amaretto
90ml water

Carefully separate the yolks and whites of 6 eggs into two large stainless steel bowls. Whisk the whites until stiff peaks form. Add 6 tablespoons caster sugar, the seeds of 1 vanilla pod and 500g mascarpone. Whisk again until smooth and thick, being careful not to over-whisk.

In a second bowl whisk the yolks until creamy, add 6 tablespoons caster sugar, the seeds of 1 vanilla pod and 500g mascarpone. Whisk again until the mixture becomes thick and velvety.

In a third bowl combine espresso shots with amaretto and the water. Quickly immerse biscuits in coffee mixture, a few at a time, then arrange in base of a mould or dish. Repeat until the base of the dish is covered.

Carefully spoon over the egg yolk mixture and smooth flat with a spatula.

Repeat another biscuit layer. Next spatula the egg white mixture on top of the biscuit layer, one last biscuit layer and finally another egg white layer.

Garnish with dark chocolate shavings or cocoa powder.

Thanks
CITRUS
+ LIMES
FARMERS MARKETS
EACH SATURDAY
SHOWGROUND
LEMONS
LIMES
LIME $2.00

Salmon with Wasabi Sweet Potato Mash

from Rainforest Foods

SERVES 1

1 piece of salmon (skin-on) or other firm-fleshed local fish
20ml macadamia oil (for frying)
sea salt to season

Mash

1 large sweet potato
1 tsp wasabi (less or more depending on your liking)
1/3 cup macadamia spread
sea salt to season

Side

1 small handful macadamias
2 aniseed myrtle leaves
½ fennel bulb
1/3 cup black turtle beans
macadamia oil (to saute)

To make the mash, cook sweet potato until soft, then mash with wasabi and macadamia spread until smooth. Season with salt.

For side, soak the beans overnight in the fridge, covered in water. The following day drain and boil until soft. Slice fennel bulbs into small pieces and roughly chop the macadamia nuts. In a frying pan, sauté aniseed myrtle and fennel for several minutes in a little oil before adding the macadamia nuts. Continue sautéing until mixture is soft, then add beans and heat through.

Heat a frying pan to high heat, add macadamia oil and place the fish in the pan, cook fish both sides to your liking. Season and serve with mash and bean mixture.

Duck Creek Macadamias

Raspberry, White Chocolate & Macadamia Cheesecake

SERVES 12

Base

1 packet (200g) plain biscuits – Scotch Finger, Granita etc
80g honey roasted macadamias
125g unsalted butter, melted

Filling

500g cream cheese, softened
½ cup caster sugar
250ml thickened cream
2 tbs lemon juice
½ tsp vanilla bean paste
3 tsp gelatine
½ cup boiling water
100g honey roasted macadamias, loosely crushed
200g white chocolate, melted
1 cup frozen raspberries

Line base and sides and lightly spray a round spring-form cake tin.

Place biscuits and macadamias in a food processor and blitz until crumbed. Add melted butter and mix until combined. Press into round tin. Chill in fridge.

Put the boiling water into a small bowl and sprinkle the gelatine over while mixing well with a fork. Set aside.

Beat the cream cheese and sugar until light and soft. Add the cream, lemon juice and vanilla bean paste and mix well. Add gelatine and mix well. It's a good idea to taste filling and add lemon juice, sugar or vanilla paste if you need it.

Fold in the melted white chocolate, raspberries and loosely crushed macadamias. Pour filling over base and chill overnight or until set.

Decorate with fresh raspberries and white chocolate flakes.

Caramelised Nut Tart

from the Macadamia Castle

MAKES 1 TART

Pastry base

38g desiccated coconut
38g almond meal
100g plain flour, sifted
100g SR flour, sifted
125g butter, softened
125g caster sugar
1 egg
½ tsp vanilla essence

Almond cream

85g butter, softened
85g caster sugar
1 whole egg and 1 yolk, beaten
20ml rum
85g almond meal
12g cornflour

Topping

230g whole macadamias
125g walnuts halves
160g almond kernels

Caramel sauce

100g caster sugar
100g golden syrup
100ml milk
100ml pure cream

In a bowl mix together all dry ingredients except the caster sugar for the base.

Cream the butter and caster sugar in a mixing bowl and beat till creamy, then add egg and vanilla and beat in well.

Add the dry mixture a little at a time and mix well. Knead the dough into a ball and wrap with cling-film, place in the fridge for at least 15 minutes.

To prepare the almond cream filling, cream the butter and sugar in a mixing bowl well with hand beaters.

Add beaten egg, yolk and rum a little at a time and mix well, add almond meal and cornflour and mix well.

Preheat the oven to 170°C.

Bring the dough to room temperature and spray a 28cm fluted tart tin well with canola spray.

Roll out base evenly to thickness of about 5mm and place carefully into prepared tart tin, trimming edges neatly.

Spike base all over with a fork and chill for 10 minutes. Then place in the preheated oven and bake for 15 minutes. Allow to cool completely, before spreading almond cream over base and bake a further 25 minutes. Leave to cool before adding topping.

Bake nuts for topping in single layer in a baking tray at 170°C for 20 minutes or until lightly browned.

To make the caramel sauce, put the sugar, syrup, milk and cream in a saucepan and cook on low heat for approximately 10 minutes, stirring until mixed then stir occasionally till thick. (HINT: The caramel is ready when the bottom of the saucepan is still visible after a spatula is swept from one side to the other).

Remove from the heat and place roasted nuts into caramel and gently mix, coating the nuts.

Gently pour caramel nuts over base of the tart, arranging with wet fingers as you go.

Allow the tart to cool in the fridge completely before slicing and serving.

Gaia Retreat's

Steamed Red Emperor Fillet

with pumpkin, edamame, seaweed, dashi broth

SERVES 4

4 x 200g fillets red emperor or other white fish such as snapper
4 x 100g kent (jap) pumpkin wedges, skin on
5cm piece ginger, sliced
1 cup edamame (soy beans), shelled
1 cup snow peas, strings removed and finely shredded
1 tbs dried wakame
1 bunch mustard greens, small leaves reserved
200ml clear fish stock
50ml mirin
50ml sake
50ml tamari sauce
furikake to serve (rice seasoning available at Asian stores) or mix shredded nori, bonito flakes and roasted sesame seeds with some sea salt

Place pumpkin and ginger in a pot and cover with cold water. Add a pinch of salt and raw sugar and simmer over a very low heat for 1 hour or until pumpkin is very soft but still holding its shape. Leave in warm liquid.

For the broth, simmer fish stock for 15 minutes with tamari, mirin, sake and a pinch of sea salt.

Steam fish for 8 minutes or until cooked through.

Gently place pumpkin in warmed bowls. Scatter dried wakame around pumpkin. Add edamame to bowls and ladle in hot broth.

Top pumpkin with steamed fish and sprinkle furikake over fish. Drape shredded snow peas and mustard greens around and over the fish. Add a few reserved small mustard leaves for garnish.

Harvest's

12-hour Braised Lamb Shoulder, Slow Roasted

SERVES 4

1.2kg lamb shoulder
50ml olive oil
1 carrot
1 onion
1 celery
3 sprigs rosemary
half bunch marjoram
500ml white wine
2 ltr chicken stock
4-6 large carrots (washed)
200g butter
1 knob ginger
1 sprig rosemary
salt
500ml yoghurt
1 bunch mint
1 lemon, juice and zest
1 bulb fennel
300g fresh peas (blanched)

Preheat oven to 90°C. Heat oil in large heavy based pan, seal shoulder on each side over high heat till golden brown. Place in oven proof dish with vegetables, wine and enough stock to all but cover the meat. Pick the herbs, reserve the leaves, place stalks in with meat. Cover with lid and cook in oven for 12 hours.

For the carrots, cook in roasting tray in the oven at 120°C, with butter, rosemary, ginger and salt for 3 hours, turning every 20 minutes until golden brown and tender.

For the mint yoghurt, pick and roughly chop the mint leaves, add to the yoghurt along with the lemon juice and zest. Add salt and mix together.

Thinly slice the fennel, either by hand or a mandelin, place in a bowl of iced water for 10 minutes and then drain thoroughly, this will stop it from oxidising and keep it crisp.

To serve, remove lamb from the baking dish, place on serving board or bowl, top with picked marjoram and rosemary. Place hot carrots in a bowl and toss with some of the mint yoghurt and then serve beside the lamb. Mix the fennel, peas and mint yoghurt, serve in a bowl on the side and finish with a touch of extra virgin olive oil.

Harvest's

Woodfired Pumpkin, Poached Eggs, Pepitas and Garden Herbs

SERVES 4

1/4 Japanese pumpkin
8 organic eggs
50ml white vinegar
1 loaf Harvest sourdough
100ml extra virgin olive oil
10g cumin seed
10g fennel seed
10g coriander seed
50g pepitas
50g sunflower seeds
salt
garden herbs, flatleaf parsley, basil, chives, mint, chervil etc.

Light your woodfired oven or if you don't have access to a woodfired oven, heat your oven to 220-240°C. Wash the pumpkin and cut into half moon shapes. Toast off all the seeds till fragrant and crush in a mortar and pestle. Place pumpkin in a bowl with spices, salt and olive oil and toss. Place on a baking tray in the oven; it will not take very long, 15 minutes; you are looking for a lot of blistering and caramelising on the outside. Remove from oven and reserve till needed.

Lightly toast the pepitas and sunflower seeds in a pan, on a medium heat.

Slice the sourdough to desired thickness and toast.

Pick, wash and dry the herbs.

Bring a medium sized pot of water to the boil, add the vinegar. Poach the eggs for 2 minutes and drain.

To serve, place the toasted sourdough on the plate, place eggs on toast and pumpkin on plate, arrange the herbs and scatter the pepita and sunflower seeds over top, finish with olive oil.

Custard with Spiced Apple and Crumble

by Harvest

SERVES 4

4 pink lady apples
100g sugar
50g butter

Custard

1 cinnamon quill
1 star anise
1 ltr cream
300g sugar
10 egg yolks

1 knob fresh ginger
1 cinnamon quill
1 star anise
1 vanilla bean
½ tsp allspice
450g butter (buerre noisette)
150g butterscotch sauce
450g rolled oats
350g hazelnut meal
250g brown sugar
pinch salt

Preheat oven too 120°C, bring cream to the boil in a small sauce pan with the spices, let infuse for 30 minutes. Whisk yolks and sugar in a bowl, bring cream to boil again and strain whilst pouring over the sugar and egg mixture, whisk thoroughly. Pour mix into an oven proof baking dish, cover and cook au bain marie in the oven for 30-40 minutes till set. Remove from oven and cool down in fridge.

For the crumble, heat the butter in a medium sauce pan, stirring constantly. The butter will foam up and when its ready, it will be a golden nutty colour and aroma. Mix all other ingredients in a bowl and pour over hot butter, mix thoroughly, place on a lined baking tray and bake in the oven at 150°C for 15 minutes till golden brown.

Peel the apples, cut in half, remove core and seeds. Place the apples, sugar and spices and toss, totally coating the apples in the sugar. Place the apples in a very hot pan with all the spices and sugar, cook until well caramelised on each side, when the sugar is getting too much colour add the butter, this will stop the sugar burning, finish in the oven for 4-5 minutes till tender.

To serve, place a spoon of the custard on each plate, place a hot apple beside the custard and cover the custard with the warm crumble.

Espresso Bean Biscotti

from the Byron Bay Coffee Company

SERVES 4

½ cup coarsely ground whole espresso beans, freshly roasted
1½ cups plain flour
2 tsp baking powder
1 tsp salt
125g chilled unsalted butter, chopped
1¼ cups almond meal
1 cup caster sugar
3 eggs, lightly whisked
½ cup freshly brewed espresso coffee
extra flour for kneading
cocoa powder for dusting
icing sugar for dusting

Preheat oven to 180°C.

Sift the flour, baking powder and salt into a large bowl. Use your fingertips to rub in the butter until it resembles breadcrumbs. Add the ground coffee beans, almond meal, caster sugar, eggs and freshly brewed coffee.

Mix well to form a soft dough, then lightly knead the dough on a floured surface, adding a little extra flour if it is too sticky, for about 2 minutes or until smooth. Divide into two equal portions.

Roll each portion into a log about 5cm in width and flatten slightly. Dust with cocoa powder and place on a baking tray lined with non-stick paper.

Bake in preheated oven for 45 minutes or until golden. Remove from oven and stand on trays for 5-10 minutes to cool slightly.

Use a sharp knife to cut the logs into 2.5cm thick slices. Place on a baking tray lined with non-stick baking paper and return to oven for 8-10 minutes, until golden brown on top.

Turn biscotti over and bake a further 8-10 minutes or until lightly golden. Remove from oven and cool on trays. Store in an airtight container for up to 4 weeks. Serve dusted with icing sugar.

honesty boxes at roadside stalls
pick up fruit, flowers, organic veggies,
coffee, honey, eggs and nuts...

Rogan Josh Pot Pies

by Zest Byron Bay

SERVES 4

175g satchel Zest Rogan Josh Recipe Base
1kg blade steak, chunkily cut
1 onion, diced
1 tbs oil
2 bay leaves
1 cup water
1 tbs cornflour
2 tbs sour cream
½ cup frozen peas
1 sheet of puff pastry
1 egg yolk

Marinate meat for 1 hour (optional).

In a heavy-based pot sauté onion in oil until soft. Add bay leaves, the meat and residue marinade. Stir on high heat for 2 minutes then add water. Lower the heat, cover and simmer for 1 hour or until the meat is tender.

Preheat the oven to 180°C.

Add 2 tablespoons water to the cornflour and stir to make a smooth paste. Add to the pot and simmer for 5 minutes until the sauce thickens.

Mix in the peas and sour cream, then spoon mixture evenly into 4 large ramekins.

Cut out pastry circles to fit the tops of the ramekins, brush egg yolk around the rims of the ramekins then gently press on the pastry circles, sealing firmly.

Brush pastry tops with remaining egg yolk and place in the oven for 10–15 minutes or until the pastry is golden brown.

Serve with a crisp green salad.

farm gate stalls,
macadamia plantations,
rows of coffee and more...

The Hinterland Track

You can spend a long time enjoying what Byron Bay has to offer and it's worth eventually heading inland. This is the stunning hinterland leg of the trip – plenty of beautiful pastoral scenery, and this time you'll see plenty of coffee and macadamia plantations too.

Heading west you'll find dozens of tiny settlements and hamlets, often with little more than a corner store, plus several historic towns like Bangalow and Eltham. Taking this trip is like opening a jewellery box, with each corner offering another roadside fruit stall or avocado vendor, every turn revealing one more small farmer producing something delicious for your basket.

Heading a bit further west you'll end up in Nimbin, famous for it's alternative hippie culture, and also a breeding ground for a new generation of farmers and producers and a great place to call it a day.

Francisco's

Marinated Olives

1kg olives, eg kalamata, Sicilian, Ligurian
300ml olive oil
1 cinnamon stick
2 tbs cumin seeds
2 tbs fennel seeds
4 bird's eye chillies, sliced lengthways
rind of 1 lemon

Dry-roast spices in a pot until fragrant over low heat, then add half the oil, chillies, lemon rind and olives and bring to the boil. Add remaining olive oil, reduce heat, cover and allow to infuse for 30 minutes. Cool in pot.

Francisco's

Quince Jam

5 quinces
4½ cups water
¼ cup lemon juice
4 cups sugar

Prepare the quince by washing and cutting in half. Working around the core, grate the flesh (including the peel) with a cheese-grater until you have about 6 cups of grated quince.

Place water in a large, wide, heavy-based saucepan and bring to the boil then add grated quince and lemon juice. Reduce heat and simmer until the quince is soft, about 10 minutes.

Add sugar and bring to back to the boil. Stir to dissolve all of the sugar. Lower heat to medium high. Cook, uncovered, stirring occasionally until quince jam turns pink and thickens to desired consistency, about 30-50 minutes.

Ladle into hot, sterilised jars and seal. Before applying the lids, sterilise them by placing them in a bowl and pouring boiling water over them. Wipe the rims of the jars clean before applying the lids.

Harvest's Dried Fruit Compote

with cinnamon, ginger & rosewater

Poaching Liquid

½ cup dried apple rings
½ cup dried apricots
½ cup dried peaches
¼ cup dried raisins
½ cup dried dates
½ cup dried figs
2 oranges, juiced and zested
15ml rosewater
200ml honey
1 ltr water
2 vanilla beans
6 cardamom pods
1 x 3cm knob fresh ginger
2 cinnamon quills
½ cup shaved roasted coconut
1 cup walnut kernels

Chop large pieces of dried fruit in half and set aside.

In heavy-based pot place all poaching liquid ingredients: scraped vanilla beans, seeds, pods, orange peel and thinly sliced ginger. Bring to boil and simmer approximately 5 minutes or until thickening and spices are fragrant.

Fold in dried fruit and cook 1–2 minutes until softened. Remove from the heat and add toasted coconut and walnuts. Cool and refrigerate.

Recommended served with cheese or warmed and eaten with ice cream.

Rita's Green Tomato Pickles

by Harvest

2kg of onions
5½ kg green tomatoes, sliced
½ cup salt
2½ kg of sugar
1 tbs mustard powder
1 tbs curry powder
1 tbs cornflour
2 tsp turmeric

Spice mixture:

30g mace
30g cloves
30g allspice
20g chilli powder
30g pepper
30g ginger powder
250ml white vinegar or apple cider vinegar

Mix all ingredients together in a food processor to form a paste. Place green tomatoes, onion and salt in a dish and stand, covered, in the fridge for 12 hours. Empty out into a large saucepan and bring to the boil. Add sugar and spice paste then simmer, uncovered, for approximately 2 hours or until a thick spooning consistency.

Combine mustard powder, curry powder, cornflour and turmeric with sufficient water to make a smooth paste. Add to pan, stirring continuously, and cook for a further 10 minutes. Pour into hot sterilised jars.

Despina's Salmon Ravioli

with rocket and parmesan

SERVES 4

1 pkt salmon, sour cream and chive ravioli from our byron farmers market stall
½ cup capers, drained
150g rocket, washed
juice of 3 lemons
100ml olive oil
100g parmesan, grated

Dry rocket in a salad spinner or with paper towels then place in a serving bowl.

Cook ravioli as per directions. On a low heat setting add olive oil to pan and add the capers. Fry for 1 minute, turn off heat and add the lemon juice. Set aside.

While still hot place ravioli on the rocket, pour over caper and lemon juice dressing and toss well. Season to taste and top with parmesan.

Bruschetta

by Coopers Shoot Tomatoes

SERVES 6

7 ripe Coopers Shoot plum tomatoes
2 cloves garlic, minced
1 red onion, finely diced
1 tbs extra virgin olive oil
1 tsp balsamic vinegar
1 tsp red wine vinegar
6 fresh basil leaves, chopped
salt and freshly ground black pepper to taste
1 baguette
¼ cup olive oil

Preheat the oven to 220C.

For the tomatoes, parboil for one minute in boiling water, drain and remove the skins. Cut them in halves or quarters, remove seeds and juice and cut out and discard the stem area.

Chop the tomatoes finely and mix with garlic, red onion, extra virgin olive oil and vinegars. Add the chopped basil then salt and pepper to taste.

Slice the baguette diagonally into slices about 2cm thick. Brush one side with olive oil and place on baking tray, olive oil-side down. Toast on top rack of oven for 5-6 minutes, until the bread just begins to turn golden brown.

Arrange the bread on a serving platter, olive oil-side up. Either place the tomato topping in a bowl separately with a spoon for people to serve themselves over the bread, or place some topping on each slice of bread and serve.

facebook.com/pages/Coopers-Shoot-Tomatoes

COUNTRY WARES
at the SHED
NEWRYBAR
NEXT

Pat's Pulled Pork

from Bangalow Sweet Pork

SERVES 6

1½ kg Bangalow Sweet Pork pork shoulder roast

The rub

¼ cup brown sugar
2 tbs seasalt
2 tbs smoked paprika
1 tbs fresh ground black pepper
½ tbs chipotle powder

Barbecue sauce

1 cup apple cider vinegar
1 cup white vinegar
3 tbs sugar
½ cup yellow mustard
¼ cup dijon mustard
½ tbs red chilli flakes
salt and pepper to taste

For the rub, mix everything together well in plastic container and set aside.

To make the sauce, combine all ingredients together and whisk until well blended.

Rub meat all over with olive oil then liberally apply the dry rub all over until meat is well covered, leaving no part of exposed meat unseasoned. Wrap in cling-film and refrigerate overnight.

The next day, remove the meat from the fridge and leave at room temperature for up to 2 hours.

On your gas barbecue, turn on one of the outside burners and heat to 120°C, maintain this temperature throughout the entire cooking time. In a double layer of aluminium foil place dry wood chips and wrap in a pouch. Punch holes in the pouch with a fork and place on the ignited burner. Position the pork shoulder as far away as possible from the heat source, close the lid and leave for 4 to 5 hours. After 5 hours check the internal temperature of the meat, aiming for 90°C. The pork shoulder will fall apart when done.

At the 5 hour mark wrap the meat tightly in double aluminium foil and return to the BBQ for another 2 hours. Unwrap and check internal temperature again and if necessary and return to the BBQ. When ready, remove and let stand, covered, for 30 to 45 minutes.

Remove the skin from the roast, discarding large pieces of fat and all bones from the meat. Pull apart with two forks or chop, then add ½ cup of the barbecue sauce, mixing in well. Add extra sauce to taste then pile high on to bread buns, adding coleslaw if desired.

Katrina Kanetani's Slow Baked Rhubarb and Strawberries

with rosemary pannacotta, champagne-vanilla jelly, elderflower sago and borage

SERVES 6

Rosemary pannacotta

300ml milk
300ml cream
85g caster sugar
8g powdered gelatine, soaked in 40ml of cold water
1½ tbs fresh rosemary, chopped

Champagne-vanilla jelly

186ml champagne /sparkling wine
1 vanilla bean, split and de-seeded
112ml sugar syrup (60g sugar and 60g water brought to the boil and simmered)
6g leaf gelatine (soaked in iced water)

Baked rhubarb

1kg rhubarb
250g sugar
zest and juice of 1 lemon
zest and juice of 1 orange
2 cinnamon sticks (broken into pieces)

Elderflower sago

1 ltr water
½ cup sago
50ml elderflower cordial
24 borage flowers (or other edible flowers)
2 tsp cocoa nibs, ground

Baked strawberries

12 strawberries
¼ cup caster sugar

For pannacotta, heat milk slowly with sugar and rosemary to infuse. Mix in the gelatine/water and the cream, then strain mixture and pour into a container to a depth of approximately 4cm and refrigerate to set.

For the jelly, warm the gelatine in a little of the sugar syrup to dissolve. Mix all ingredients together and set in a container, in the refrigerator, 4cm deep.

To prepare the rhubarb, peel the rhubarb, then place the peel on the bottom of a 25 x 30cm baking tray. Cut half of the rhubarb sticks into 3cm lengths and the remaining half into 6cm lengths and place on top of the peel in the baking tray. Sprinkle sugar, zest and juices over rhubarb and add the cinnamon sticks. Cover tray with foil and bake slowly at 125°C for 15–25 minutes. Place in clean tray in fridge to cool.

Cut the longer rhubarb pieces in half lengthwise and set aside. Strain juices into a pan and reduce over a low heat to thicken slightly. Set aside.

For sago, bring water to the boil, add the sago and boil for approximately 12 minutes (there should still be a white centre in the sago when it is cooked). Strain under cold running water, then drain. Place in container and add the elderflower cordial. Set aside.

For strawberries, halve and toss in a bowl with the sugar. Place on a paper-lined baking tray and bake at 170°C for 5 minutes. Remove and set aside.

To serve, place 2 small rhubarb pieces standing up, and 3 long rhubarb pieces on each plate. Place 3 baked strawberry halves beside the rhubarb. Place 2 spoons each of the jelly and the pannacotta at different angles on the plate next to the rhubarb and strawberries. Divide sago evenly between the 6 plates, sprinkling over and around the rhubarb, strawberries, pannacotta and jelly. Spoon the sauce over the rhubarb and strawberries. Sprinkle over a little of the ground cocoa nibs and place 4 borage flowers over each dessert and serve.

The Bangalow Dining Rooms Organic Chicken Liver Parfait

with apple gel and mini sourdough loaf

SERVES 4

Parfait

900g organic chicken livers
20g sea salt
30g green peppercorns
550g butter, melted
100g onion, finely diced
20g garlic, minced
3 bay leaves
2 sprigs thyme
200m dry vermouth
90ml port wine
90ml brandy
2 eggs

Apple gel

4 granny smith apples
10g salt
800ml water
100g sugar
30ml cider vinegar

Preheat the oven to 150°C. Clean the livers of any fat and place in a bowl with salt and peppercorns. Sweat onions, garlic, thyme and bay leaves in 50g of the butter over a low heat until very soft – do not allow them to colour. Add vermouth, port and brandy and reduce by half. Strain and cool then blend together with livers, remaining butter and eggs in a liquidiser until smooth. Pass through a fine strainer.

Line a terrine mould with two layers of cling-film then pour mixture into the mould.

Cover with lid or foil. Place into bain-marie (water bath) and then into oven, turning oven down to 110°C . Cook until internal temperature reaches 68°C .

Serve with apple gel and sourdough loaf.

For apple gel, place apples, salt and water into a saucepan, bring to the boil then simmer for 30 minutes or until very soft and apples have fallen apart. Pass through a fine strainer. Meanwhile, place an empty plate in freezer for gel-testing. Return 400ml of apple liquid into a pot with sugar and vinegar, bring to the boil then reduce to a simmer for about half an hour or until gel forms when a small spoonful of mixture is placed on cold plate.

385

Sunforest

SIMPLE
PLEASURES
Nachos
-Chicken Salad wrap $8
-Bean Salad wrap $8

The Loft's Baked Rhubarb Custard

with ginger granita

SERVES 6

Poached rhubarb

1 bunch of ripe washed rhubarb, sliced 5cm long
2 cups caster sugar
peel from 1 orange
1 cinnamon quill

Ginger granita

Ginger granita
125g caster sugar
80g fresh ginger coarsely chopped
1 tbs lemon juice

Baked vanilla cream

675ml pouring cream
½ vanilla bean, split and seeds scraped
105g caster sugar
6 egg yolks

For rhubarb, place all ingredients in a bowl and mix by hand until well combined. Place in a baking tray and cover with foil then bake for approximately 40 minutes at 175°C until rhubarb is soft and deep pink in colour.

For ginger granita, combine sugar, ginger and 600ml water in a small saucepan over medium heat, stirring to dissolve sugar. Increase the heat to high and bring to the boil. Remove from heat, cover and stand to infuse for 20 minutes. Strain through a fine sieve, pressing on the ginger to remove as much liquid as possible (discard ginger), then add lemon juice. Pour into a shallow tray, transfer to freezer and stir occasionally with a fork until frozen and ice crystals form (3-6 hours).

To make the baked vanilla cream, preheat oven to 160°C. Combine cream and vanilla in a saucepan over medium heat and stir occasionally until hot (5 minutes). Remove from heat, cover and stand to infuse for 1 hour. Whisk sugar and yolks in a bowl until pale and creamy. Reheat cream over medium heat until hot then gradually pour onto yolk mixture, gently stirring to combine. Strain through a fine sieve into a jug (discard vanilla bean). Stand for 5 minutes then skim foam from surface. Divide evenly among six 250ml ovenproof glasses. Place glasses on a folded tea towel placed in a deep roasting tray, ensuring they are sitting flat. Fill pan with enough hot water to come two-thirds of the way up the sides of glasses and cover with foil. Pierce a few holes in foil with a skewer to release steam, then bake until set, but with a slight wobble (30-35 minutes). Remove from oven, remove foil and stand in water until cool (30-40 minutes). Remove from water, dry glasses and refrigerate until chilled and firm (2 hours).

To serve, sit chilled rhubarb pieces on top of the set cream and place a spoonful of granita crystals on top.

NIMBIN

Nimbin Valley Cheeses

Five generations of dairy farming combined with stunning surrounds, and the happiest animals lead to the creation of the best goat and cow milk cheeses in Australia by Nimbin Valley Dairy.

Blue Cow and Blue Goat

These two cheeses are characteristic of the milder firm blues from Europe like Gorgonzola. Salty and packed with savoury flavours they will stand up to malty beers like Stone and Wood Jasper Ale. They develop fruity notes from about 12 weeks of age which marry well with sweet fruits.

White Cow and White Goat

Made in the style of a raw milk Camembert de Normandie both of these cheeses are about as close as it gets in Australia to a raw milk soft cheese. A complex mix of lactic acid bacteria, yeasts and moulds to recreate the complex raw milk environment resulting in deep rich flavours. Great on crusty bread with any of the lighter wines.

Sweet Goat

This is the stand out semi hard goat cheese. Perfect as a table cheese eaten with crackers; loads of flavour that lasts on the palate.

Monte Nardi

After spending time with some of the early local Italian settlers in the Northern Rivers region we wanted to recreate the style of cheese that was made when they first arrived - and this is it! Perfect as a table cheese but also lovely grated on pasta.

Washed Cow and Washed Goat

The Trappist monks of France used to wash their cheeses in brine to maintain the rind. This washing encouraged the growth of microflora which added a pungency to the cheese paste. Beautiful with Chardonnay and crusty bread, the White Goat is truly a unique cheese in this country.

Sainte Billie

A chance visit from a French Cheesemaker, Pascal Destandau and his partner Eric, resulted in the development of a cheese which they used to make in California. Similar to the classic lactic goat cheeses of southern France, it displays beautiful goaty notes with a complex long flavour. Pairs very well with Beaujolais or any of the lighter style reds.

nimbinvalley.com.au

Byron Bay Cheese Company

Perfect Cheese Platter

When these cheeses were made all the rules were broken. Many years of hard work perfecting the classic artisan techniques of French and Italian cheese makers were employed. In the spirit of freedom that comes from growing up in a region bursting with a counter cultural vibe the cheeses were all mixed up to create something unique, cheeses that reflect the beautiful rich soils and pastures of the Byron hinterland.

Brooklet Brie

A modern interpretation of the classic Brie de Meaux. It has a soft and creamy paste with a beautiful pure white rind and perfect with fresh sourdough.

Nashua Washed Rind

A pungent soft cheese with a vibrant rind reminiscent of the Italian Tallegio. Notes of cauliflower and fresh grass are carried by the luscious rich paste. Like many washed rinds the flavour is much less intense than the aroma so be brave and dive in! Perfect on a mild wholemeal or rye bread or a simple water cracker.

Tintenbar Triple Cream

The créme de la créme of bloomy white mould cheeses. Full of beautifully rich local cream this is a cheese that can stand alone. Gooey and luscious it will work well on most breads and crackers.

The perfect cheese platter

To make the perfect cheese platter with these cheeses allow about 30-40g per person and add some crisp green apple, honeycomb or dried muscatel grapes, the apple helps cleanse the palate while the sweetness of the grapes or honeycomb will add a contrast to the richness of the cheeses, perfect served with lavosh bread.

Remove them from the fridge about half an hour before serving and remember to place some baking paper or similar under the cheeses if using a wooden chopping board to reduce the chance of any taints.

The Nashua is robust enough to cope with a red wine but the others are best with crisp white wines, although there are no rules in this part of the world so enjoy them with your favourite wine, cider or even beer!

Byron Bay Writers' Festival

Tiny Herbie Tarts

SERVES 6

18 slices of white bread, crusts removed
4 tbs softened butter
2 eggs
2 tbs milk
½ cup cream
2 tsp chopped chives
1 tsp each of dill, thyme and parsley
2 tbs grated parmesan

Preheat the oven to 210°C.

Brush 2 x 12 cup muffin pans with melted butter. Cut the bread into rounds with a biscuit cutter, then flatten each round with a rolling pin. Butter both sides of the rounds and press into the muffin pans. Bake for 10 minutes until brown and crisp. Reduce heat to 180°C.

Combine eggs, milk, cream and herbs and mix well. Pour into bread cases and sprinkle with parmesan. Bake for 25 minutes or until filling is lightly browned and set. Eat immediately.

Wood-Fired Moroccan Spiced Lamb Pot Pie

by the Eltham Hotel

SERVES 4-6

Moroccan spice mix

¼ cup each: coriander, cumin seed, sumac and cinnamon
2 tsp chilli flakes
1 tsp cardamom

Lamb pie filling

1½ -2kg lamb shoulder, boned
100ml vegetable oil
Moroccan spice mix seasoning
2 eggplants, halved lengthways
olive oil
1 head of garlic, top sliced off
1 large red onion, grated
5 garlic cloves thinly sliced
1 tsp fresh ginger, finely grated
1 tsp turmeric
2 tsp sweet paprika
2 tsp ground cumin
½ tsp cayenne pepper
pinch of saffron in warm water
1 cup crushed tomatoes
½ bunch flatleaf parsley, chopped
bunch coriander leaves, chopped
5 vine-ripened tomatoes, diced
seasalt and pinch of sugar
juice of 1 lemon
6 sheets of puff pastry
2 eggs, lightly beaten

To make the Moroccan spice mix, grind ingredients in a spice grinder or mortar and pestle. Sift into a large bowl and discard the large spices that remain in sieve.

For the pie, add 100ml vegetable oil to the spice mix to make a paste and rub onto the lamb shoulder.

Cover with cling-film and refrigerate for a minimum of 2 hours but preferably overnight. Bake in a wood-fired oven or regular oven at 150°C for 3 hours, or until fork-tender. Leave aside to cool then shred the lamb or cut into chunks.

Drizzle the eggplant and garlic cloves with olive oil and place in a moderate oven until golden brown and the flesh of the eggplant is soft. Scoop out, squeeze garlic from skins then mash together the eggplant and roasted garlic, discarding skins.

In a heavy-based pot, place red onion, garlic, ginger, turmeric, paprika, cumin, cayenne pepper and a tablespoon of olive oil and fry until fragrant. Add saffron water, crushed tomatoes, parsley and coriander.

Leave on a moderate heat and simmer. Add the shredded roast lamb.

In a separate pan with 2 tablespoons olive oil, add diced tomatoes, 1 teaspoon salt and the sugar and cook over a medium-high heat, stirring frequently, for about 5 minutes or until most of the moisture has evaporated. Add mashed eggplant and cook on a very low heat, stirring frequently, for about 20 minutes or until most of the mixture is very thick. Remove from the heat and stir in the lemon juice and small handful of chopped parsley.

To assemble the pie, place the tomato and lamb mixture in the bottom of your pie ramekin to 2/3 full. Spoon the eggplant mixture on the top to fill and top with a pastry lid. Use a fork to secure the edges and brush with egg. Place in a moderate oven for 15 minutes until puffed and golden brown.

Serve with a roasted eggplant, garlic and potato puree and green beans, or couscous and herbed raita.

Christie Connelly's

Smoked Salmon Crepe Sushi

MAKES 48 PIECES

Crepes

150g plain flour
250ml milk
2 eggs
pinch of salt
vegetable oil for frying

Filling

250g cream cheese
2 tsp wasabi paste
1 tbs soy sauce
3 tbs sesame seeds
2 finger limes, flesh scooped out (about 2 tbs)
500g smoked salmon
6 nori sheets (roasted seaweed)
pickled ginger, to serve

For the crepes, place flour, milk, eggs and salt into a large bowl and whisk until combined. Set aside for 30 minutes at room temperature. Heat a 20cm frypan and brush with a little vegetable oil. Ladle in some crepe batter and swirl the pan so that it just coats the bottom in a thin, even layer. When small bubbles appear on the surface, after about 30 seconds, flip and cook for a further 20 seconds. Transfer to a plate and repeat with the remaining batter to make 6 crepes. Chill in the fridge until completely cold.

For the filling, place cream cheese, wasabi paste, soy sauce, sesame seeds and finger lime flesh into a bowl and beat until well combined. Chill until crepes are ready.

To assemble, place a crepe on to a plate and spread evenly with the cream cheese mixture. Top with slices of smoked salmon and finally a sheet of nori. Carefully and firmly roll up then slice into 8 neat rounds and serve with pickled ginger and extra soy and wasabi.

Doma's Seared Salmon Sashimi Salad

with ponzu and umeboshi basil pesto

SERVES 4

500g sashimi-grade salmon
½ tsp fine sea salt
100g shredded daikon radish
¼ cup shredded red capsicum
¼ cup shredded yellow capsicum
¼ cup chives cut in 3cm lengths
¼ cup dill
160g mesclun lettuce
¼ cup edible flower petals
lemon wedges

Lemon dressing

50ml lemon juice
100ml olive oil

Ponzu sauce

225ml lemon juice
25ml orange juice
50ml rice vinegar
100ml soy sauce
50ml mirin (evaporate alcohol)
5g shredded bonito flake

Umeboshi basil pesto

2pc umeboshi (salted plum)
25g basil leaves
20g pine nuts
1 tsp rice vinegar
2 tsp mirin
100ml grapeseed oil

To make the ponzu sauce, combine all ingredients and a pinch of salt and refrigerate overnight if possible.

Blend all ingredients for umeboshi basil pesto together in a blender.

Take the skin off the salmon and season with sea salt then sear over open flame or in a pan over high heat for 15 seconds each side just to slightly cook surface.

To serve, cut salmon finely into 5mm thick slices and place on each plate.

Strain the ponzu sauce and pour over the fish.

Dot the umeboshi basil pesto around the salmon.

Top with mesclun lettuce, daikon, capsicum, herbs and edible flower petals.

Pour the lemon dressing over the salad and place lemon wedges on the side.

Splendour in the Grass Fish Pie

MAKES 1 PIE

50g butter
1 large leek, white and pale green part finely sliced
30g plain flour
50ml white wine
30ml lemon juice
170ml (2/3 cup) thickened cream
salt and pepper, to taste
700g white fish fillets (without skin or bones) cut into bite-sized pieces
30g (1/3 cup) grated parmesan
1-2 tbs finely chopped parsley
2 sheets frozen puff pastry, thawed (use sheets that measure about 25cm by 25cm)

Preheat the oven to 210°C.

Melt the butter in a large saucepan over medium heat and add the leek and cook for a few minutes until softened, stirring occasionally. Keep the heat low to avoid browning of the leek.

Add flour to the pan and cook over medium heat, stirring, for about one minute.

Stir in the white wine and lemon juice, then add cream and cook, stirring occasionally, until sauce simmers and thickens. Season with salt and pepper.

Add fish pieces, parmesan cheese and parsley to the pan and stir gently until just combined. Remove from the heat. The filling may seem slightly dry at this stage, but the fish will release a lot of moisture as it cooks in the oven.

Using a 1 litre capacity baking dish as a guide, cut the pie lid from the pastry sheets, cutting about 1-2 cm larger than the baking dish.

You may need to join two sheets of pastry to cover the dish. Overlap the two sheets of pastry about 1.5cm and press together to join.

Place filling mixture into the baking dish, cover with the pastry sheets and bake the pie for about 40 minutes.

Sublime Pear and Almond Tart with Habanero Apricot Glaze

Byron Bay Chilli Company

SERVES 12

1 medium frozen tart shell
1½ cups almonds
¾ cup sugar
60 g softened butter
2 tbs flour
2 tsp almond essence
3 tbs Amaretto, Frangelico or cream
2 eggs
4 firm medium sized pears
1 cup apricot jam
1-2 tbs Byron Bay Chilli Heavenly Habanerno sauce
2 tbs toasted slivered almonds
whipped cream to serve

Gently heat and stir the apricot jam and Heavenly Habanero Chilli sauce together in a small saucepan. Once done, set aside to cool.

In a food processor, grind almonds until very fine. Add sugar, butter, flour, essence, liqueur or cream and eggs. Blend until smooth.

Remove tart shell from freezer and brush the base with half of the jam mixture. Pour almond filling over jam and refrigerate tart while preparing pears.

Peel the pears, core and slice thickly. Arrange pears on top of almond filling in a circular pattern, saving a few slices for the center.

Bake the tart at 180°C for 1 hour or until filling is set and lightly browned.

While the tart is still warm, spread with remaining apricot jam mixture and sprinkle with toasted almonds. Allow tart to cool.

Serve with whipped cream on the side, and if you like a little extra hot sauce.

Crystal Castle and Shambhala Garden's

Vegan Banana and Pecan Cake

SERVES 12

4 cups self-raising flour
2 cups caster sugar
2 cups chopped pecans
5 ripe bananas (2 mashed, 3 chopped)
1 cup oil 375ml apple juice
1 cup soy milk
½ cup coconut syrup
and a whole lot of love

Icing

4 cups almond meal
2 cups icing sugar mixture
4-6 tbs Nuttelex
3 tbs soya milk to blend

Garnish

1½ cups flaked almonds, toasted
¼ cup pecan halves
¼ cup goji berries
¼ cup blueberries

Preheat oven to 165°C. Grease and line with baking paper a 28cm round cake tin. In a bowl combine flour, sugar and pecans. In a separate bowl mix apple juice, soy milk, oil and syrup together then stir through bananas. Slowly add dry ingredients to wet mixture until well combined. Spoon batter into baking pan and bake for an hour.

For icing, blend the almond meal, icing sugar and Nuttelex in a blender. Slowly add soya milk until you have the right consistency. When the cake is cool, ice all over and garnish with nuts and berries.

Rock and Roll's

Womlette

SERVES 1-2

Omelette

3 eggs
1 cup shredded wombok
"Mega Chef" light soy sauce (gluten-free)
vegetable oil

Salad

6 cherry tomatoes, halved
telegraph cucumbers, sliced
coriander sprig, picked
mint sprigs, picked
bean sprouts, washed
carrot, grated

Chilli garlic sauce

1 cup Sriracha sauce
3 cloves garlic, finely diced
3 coriander roots, cleaned

Ajard (Asian dressing)

½ cup sugar
½ cup white vinegar

Dissolve dressing ingredients in a pot over medium heat then allow to cool.

For the omelette, whisk eggs in a bowl while heating a small pan to medium high. Add enough oil to the pan to cover the bottom and sides (5mm). Wait 10 seconds or so until the oil starts to shimmer. Tip egg mix gently into the centre of the pan so that it cooks in the oil and does not catch on the sides of the pan. Shake the pan around softly and push eggs in to create texture. Add shredded wombok and push into the cooking egg, then carefully flip the dish. Once flipped, turn heat down to low and cook 1 minute to caramelise the wombok. Flip again and season with soy sauce.

Slide out the Womlette on to paper towel, then roll like a cigar inside the paper towel and let it rest.

While it rests, combine the salad ingredients and dress with some ajard.

To assemble, unwrap the Womlette, smear chilli sauce on serving plate, cut the Womlette in half and place on top of the chilli. Throw salad on top and serve.

facebook.com/RockAndRollCafeMullumbimby

Shelley Craft's

Byron Breakfast Smoothie

SERVES 1

6 strawberries
1 cup blueberries
1 cup raspberries
1 banana
2 tbs yoghurt
1 tsp honey
2 tbs Byron Bay muesli
1 cup milk

Place the strawberries, blueberries, raspberries and banana with the honey, yoghurt, muesli and milk in a blender and blend till smooth.

Mix in the muesli and enjoy.

Mullum Music Festival Zest Butter Chicken

SERVES 4-6 WITH RICE AND ACCOMPANIMENTS

175g Zest Butter Chicken Blend
1kg chicken thighs
2 tbs oil
1 onion, diced
¾ cup stock or water
1 bay leaf
100g tomato paste
3 tbs almond meal
3 tbs plain yoghurt or sour cream

Cut the chicken into chunks and marinate with Zest Butter Chicken Blend for at least 1 hour in the fridge if possible.

In a heavy-based pot, cook the onions until soft, then add chicken and cook for 2 minutes on high.

Add tomato paste, bayleaf, almond meal and stock or water, stirring well.

Bring to the boil, lower the heat and simmer for 15 minutes or until just cooked.

Add yoghurt or sour cream and simmer for 5 minutes. Reduce sauce if necessary.

Serve with rice.

The Retro Shop
BANGALOW

OPEN

PREMIUM

Terase Davidson's

Asian Inspired Pork Belly Salad

SERVES 4-6

1kg Bangalow sweet pork belly, skin on, bone out

Braising liquid

1 knob ginger, roughly chopped
3 star anise
3 cloves
1 cinnamon quill
3 long red chillies, roughly chopped
6 kaffir lime leaves
1 lemongrass, white part only, roughly chopped
2 tbs oyster sauce
2 tbs ketchup manis
4 tbs soy sauce

Salad

2 bunches coriander
1 bunch mint
1/2 bunch Vietnamese mint
1 telegraph cucumber, deseeded and julienned
2 granny smith apples, julienned
1/3 cup sesame seeds, lightly toasted

Dressing

1/2 cup caster sugar
1 1/2 cups cold water
5 long red chillis, deseed and julienned
1 knob ginger, peel and julienned
2-3 limes, juice only
1 tsp white wine vinegar
3-4 limes garnish

Place pork belly in a large ovenproof pot, skin side up. Cover with cold water until water is approx 3cm over the pork. Place all braising liquid ingredients in the pot and stir to combine.

Place pot on the stove on high heat and bring to the boil, reduce to simmer then skim off residue with a ladle and disgard. Cut out a piece of baking paper to fit the surface of the pot, place lid on the pot and allow to gently simmer on the stove top for approx 2-3 hours or until pork is 'pull apart tender'.

Allow the pork belly to rest in the liquid with the lid off for 30 minutes. Remove the baking paper.

For the dressing, place the sugar and water in a nonstick fry pan and stir to dissolve the sugar, then bring to the boil and allow to reduce by a quarter before carefully adding your chilli and ginger, continue to boil until reduced by another quarter and the liquid has thickened and appears 'glossy'. Remove from the heat and allow to cool.

Once the dressing is cool, stir in the lime juice and white wine vinegar, taste, and add more lime juice if you need more sour flavour.

Carefully remove the pork belly from the braising liquid with a pair of tongs, pull apart the pork belly into long threads, discard the skin and any of the fat.

In a large bowl, gently combine the salad ingredients with the pork belly using your hands, drizzle over the dressing (keep some dressing in reserve) then mix again to coat the salad in the dressing - you can also drizzle over some of the braising liquid if you'd like, finish by drizzling over the remaining dressing and scatter over the toasted sesame seeds.

This recipe is great for taking to BBQs and picnics, simply keep all the ingredients separate and combine together just before serving.

For this dish the pork is best served at room temperature.

Organic Passion's

Chocolate, Rosewater and Berry Trifle

SERVES 6

Gluten-free, vegan chocolate sponge cake

1 cup almond meal
½ cup desiccated coconut
1 cup gluten-free self raising flour
1½ cups coconut sugar
150ml macadamia oil
400ml ½ water and ½ soya milk – or milk of your choice
6 tsp gluten-free baking powder
2 tbs balsamic vinegar
¾ cup cocoa powder
2 tsp vanilla paste
1 tsp salt

Chocolate rosewater sauce

½ cup agave
½ cup raw cacao powder
½ cup water
2 tsp vanilla
2–4 tbs rosewater (or to taste)

Coconut lime custard

1ltr coconut cream
zest of 2 limes and juice of 1
¼ cup light agave syrup
2 tsp vanilla
½ tsp salt
2 tbs arrowroot powder (thickener)
1 tsp agar agar (setting agent)

Fruit layers

1 punnet (100g) blueberries
1 punnet (150g) strawberries, sliced into quarters

Garnish

½ cup macadamia nuts, roughly chopped
70% organic dark chocolate, shaved

For the sponge cake, mix together all the dry ingredients.

Make a well in the centre and in it place the vanilla paste, macadamia oil and balsamic vinegar. Gradually add the milk/water combination, beating it gently into the batter. Pour into a lined flat tray about 3cm deep.

For the sauce, whisk all the ingredients together into a thinnish paste. As it sits, it will thicken. For best results leave overnight.

For the custard, bring the coconut cream to a gentle boil (just under boiling) then add lime zest and juice, agave, vanilla and salt and stir. Separately, combine agar agar and arrowroot powder, add a little water and mix to form a loose paste. Slowly stir into coconut mixture and continue stirring for about three minutes to dissolve agar agar. Place in the fridge to cool and set.

To assemble the trifle, place a little drizzle of chocolate rosewater sauce on the bottom of the glass, then a little coconut custard. Break off some cake and place that in the glass then more custard and sauce and some of the berries. Sprinkle macadamias and shaved chocolate between each layer. Repeat until you reach the final layer and finish with lots of berries, chocolate shavings and macadamia nuts on the top.

100 Mile Table

Harissa Chicken with Caramelised Orange and Pomegranate

SERVES 4

1 x 1.6kg Alstonville chicken, cut into 10 pieces
coriander sprigs, to serve

Harissa

6 dried long red chillies
½ sm red capsicum, de-seeded
2 fresh long red chillies, de-seeded
2 sm hot chillies
30g garlic, crushed
1 tsp ground cumin
1 tsp ground coriander
sea salt, to taste
150ml extra virgin olive oil

Orange and pomegranate dressing

8 tbs caster sugar
4 oranges, peeled and each cut into 3 thick slices
juice of 2 limes
sea salt and freshly ground pepper
good splash of Brookfarm lime and chilli macadamia oil
4 tbs pomegranate seeds

To make the harissa, soak the dried chillies in hot water for about 20-30 minutes or until soft. Drain and squeeze out excess liquid. Place all ingredients in a blender and blend to a rough paste.

Crust the chicken pieces liberally in the harissa (any extra can be kept in an airtight jar in the fridge for up to a month). Heat a heavy-based fry pan or grill plate, add a splash of olive oil and grill the chicken until well caramelised and just cooked through. You may need to finish the chicken in a medium oven for a few minutes, depending on the size.

If you get the chance, the chicken can be marinated a day ahead.

Meanwhile, to make the dressing, add the caster sugar to a heavy-based wide skillet and heat. As the sugar starts to melt, add the orange slices and lay flat without overlapping. Turn the oranges on a regular basis, being careful not to break them up too much, until they are well caramelised on both sides and starting to blacken. Before the caramel cooks too far, add the lime juice and salt and pepper and stir well. Remove from the heat and set aside.

When the chicken is cooked, arrange the pieces on a large platter.

Return the orange dressing to a medium heat until just bubbling. Remove from the heat and add a good splash of macadamia oil. Check the seasoning to ensure the dressing is well balanced. You may want to add more lime juice at this point.

Add the pomegranate seeds. Pour the oranges and dressing over the chicken and sprinkle with coriander to serve.

Serve with steamed couscous and a sharp preserved lemon salsa.

Open Table's

Kunafa with Tangelo Clove Syrup

Garnished with pistachio and pomegranate

SERVES 12-16

Syrup

200g brown sugar / Rapadura sugar / dehydrated coconut sugar
1 cup of tangelo juice
1 tsp of orange blossom essence
1 lemon squeezed and juiced

Kunafa

200g ghee / clarified butter
200g Kunafa noodles (find in Middle Eastern shops)
350g fresh ricotta and hard goat cheese
100g pecans / hazelnuts / chestnuts

Garnish

pistachio and pomegranate kernels

To make syrup, mix up the sugar with tangelo juice and clove, let it come to a point of boiling.

Add the orange essence and lemon juice mixes and cook till it reaches syrup texture.

Reheat before pouring it onto the Kunafa.

To make the Kunafa, make sure to separate the noodles and fluff them up in order for it to soak evenly in the ghee while cooking.

Place on medium heat a frying pan (24 cm diameter), pour in half the amount of ghee, let it melt and top with half the amount of the noodles while arranging and aerating, cook for 2-3 minutes.

Crumble over the ricotta and goat cheese and sprinkle with chopped pecans (or other nuts). Cover with remaining noodles and press firmly. Fry while rotating the pan in such a way where the noodles move freely.

Check the bottom part of the noodles from time to time with a wide spatula, until golden.

Cover the top of the frying pan with a big flat plate and turn carefully to see the cooked side. Put the remaining ghee in the pan and smooth the noodles back to frying the other side in the same way.

After cooking the top of the noodles to a unified golden crust, remove from heat. Carefully transfer to a large serving dish and pour over the festive and reheated tangelo clove syrup. Sprinkle with ground pistachios and pomegranate kernel to serve.

be sure to visit one of
our local authentic
farmers markets

Green Tea Noodles with Mushrooms

from the Witches Broomstick

SERVES 4

400g green tea noodles, blanched till al dente
peanut oil, for cooking
2 king oyster mushrooms
12 lge shiitake mushrooms, stems removed
12 regular oyster mushrooms
5cm knob fresh ginger, peeled and grated
2 long red chillies, de-seeded, cut into julienne
4 shallots, finely sliced
8 snow peas
1 cup mirin
1 cup light soy sauce
2 tsp sesame oil
4 tbs caster sugar

To prepare the mushrooms, cut each king oyster in half width-wise, slice the meaty bottom pieces in half lengthways them slice each piece finely along the length; finely slice the shiitakes; tear each oyster mushroom into 2 or 3 pieces.

Mix the mirin, soy, sesame oil and caster sugar together and set aside.

Heat a large wok till it smokes and add a good splash of peanut oil (you could also use a great macadamia oil). Add the mushrooms and stir-fry until just soft, remove from the wok and set aside.

And another splash of peanut oil to the wok. Add the ginger, chilli, shallots and snow peas. Stir-fry till fragrant, about 2 minutes.

Return the mushrooms to the wok then add the seasonings. As soon as the liquid boils, toss through the noodles to combine and serve immediately in 4 bowls.

byronfarmersmarket.com.au/farmers/view/25

Shannon Fricke's

Aromatic Chicken Tagine

SERVES 5

1 whole organic chicken, jointed, or chicken pieces (skin on)
2 fennel bulbs
2 red onions, peeled and roughly chopped
4 organic garlic cloves, squashed and roughly chopped
1 sm bunch coriander, roughly torn
200g green olives
pinch saffron threads
lemon rind, roughly peeled
pinch ground ginger, cumin, sea salt and pepper
1ltr chicken stock

Make an aromatic rub for the chicken, mixing the saffron threads, ground ginger, cumin, sea salt and pepper in a small bowl then run generously over the chicken skin. Place chicken pieces in a bowl, cover with cling-film and pop in the fridge for a couple of hours or even better overnight.

Heat the oven to 150°C and leave to warm.

On the stovetop, heat some oil in a tagine or casserole dish and fry the chicken pieces over medium heat until the skin becomes crispy. Add the fennel bulbs, red onions, garlic, lemon rind and coriander and olives fry until the ingredients soften. Cover in chicken stock, pop on the lid or cover with aluminium foil–and pop in the oven to slow cook for 2 hours. Check the meat falls away from the bone, and if so, you know it's ready.

Serve with warm, fluffy cous cous.

LE CREUSET

Tamsin Holloway's

Soba Noodles with Ponzu Dressing

SERVES 4

50g sesame seeds
pinch of salt
250g Soba noodles
5 spring onions, finely sliced

Ponzu dressing

½ cup lime juice
4 tbs black rice vinegar
2 tbs soy sauce
4 tbs mirin
2 tsp caster sugar
2 tsp sesame oil

Toast the sesame seeds in a dry frying pan, over high heat until golden brown then pour into a bowl and set aside.

Prepare a large bowl of iced water, to plunge the Soba noodles once cooked and drained.

Bring a large saucepan of water to the boil with the salt and add the Soba noodles. Cook for approximately 6 minutes until just tender, drain, then plunge into the iced water until cooled then drain again.

Meanwhile, pour the Ponzu ingredients into a jar with a tightly fitting lid and shake vigorously to combine.

Place the Soba noodles in a large bowl, pour half the Ponzu dressing over the noodles and sprinkle with the spring onions. Toss to combine.

Set aside for 30 minutes to allow flavours to develop.

Serve with the remaining Ponzu dressing drizzled over the top and sprinkle with the toasted sesame seeds.

*Variations – this dish can be served hot or cold but is typically served cold. You can add left-over shredded pork etc.

Fishmonger's Snapper

with a citrus chilli marinade on fragrant rice

SERVES 4

4 x 160g portions of fresh, locally caught snapper fillets

Marinade

juice and zest of 1 large orange
juice and zest of 2 limes
1 long red chilli, de-seeded and roughly chopped
1 tbs fresh tarragon, roughly chopped
1 tbs spring onions, roughly chopped
1 tbs nutmeg
4 tbs canola oil
2 tbs extra virgin olive oil
dash of Worcestershire sauce
pinch of salt and pepper

Garnish

½ red capsicum, julienned
60g bean sprouts
flat leaf parsley, finely diced

Fragrant rice

400g jasmine rice
600ml water
½ bunch coriander roots (rinsed well)
½ stalk lemongrass
50ml extra virgin olive oil
50ml fish sauce

Combine snapper fillets with marinade then leave to marinate for a minimum of 2 hours.

Blend Worcestershire sauce with salt and pepper in a food processor.

Blitz and slowly add canola and olive oil.

Cook on barbecue or grill on high heat for 90 seconds each side

Serve on a bed of Fragrant Rice and garnish with bean sprouts, capsicum and parsley,

Combine the rice, water, coriander roots and lemongrass and cook the rice until the water is absorbed.

Remove coriander roots and lemongrass and mix in oil and fish sauce.

Traditional Thai's Coconut-Braised Beef Ribs

with Penang Curry

SERVES 10

1.5kg short beef ribs cut horizontally by the butcher
oyster sauce for marinating

Braising liquid

1 tin coconut milk
1ltr water
30ml oyster sauce
50ml fish sauce
100g palm sugar
5 kaffir lime leaves
1 sm knob of galangal, crushed or sliced
2 stalks lemongrass, lightly crushed
2 large red chillies, sliced in half
5 coriander roots, washed and crushed

Curry paste

1mediumred onion
5 long red chillies
100g peeled garlic
50g dried red chillies, deseeded and soaked in water
50g galangal
30g turmeric
30g lemongrass
roasted coriander seeds
roasted cumin seeds
shrimp paste
2 tbs curry paste
vegetable oil
70g palm sugar
50ml fish sauce
1 cup roasted peanuts, crushed
800ml coconut water mix (1 part coconut cream and milk to 2 parts water)
2 kaffir lime leaves
sliced bamboo
baby corn
snakebeans (or green beans)
handful of Thai basil

For the braising liquid, mix coconut milk, water, oyster sauce, fish sauce and palm sugar in braising pan. Add kaffir lime leaves, galangal, lemongrass, chillies and coriander roots.

Coat beef ribs in oyster sauce and marinate 3 hours. Heat vegetable oil in a wok and deep-fry ribs. While warm place them in pan with braising liquid then cover dish with grease-proof paper and a lid. Braise the ribs at 220°C for 2 hours, then braise at 180°C for another 2 hours or until the meat pulls off the bone. Once cooked set aside to cool and when cold rest in the fridge overnight.

For curry paste, blend all ingredients together except for the coriander, cumin seeds and shrimp paste. In a spice grinder grind the coriander and cumin seeds then add to blended paste. Add the shrimp paste.

On medium heat, cook curry paste in vegetable oil, stirring consistently until fragrant (about 20 minutes). Add palm sugar and caramelise for around 2 minutes. Add the fish sauce and ½ cup peanuts and cook for another 2 minutes. Pour in approximately 500ml of the coconut water mix – the consistency of the curry should be rather thick. Adjust the thickness of the curry to your liking by adding extra coconut water mix.

Add bamboo, baby corn and snakebeans and cook for a few minutes.

Separately grill beef ribs and add to the curry. Add Thai basil before serving and garnish with the remaining ½ cup of peanuts.

Traditional Thai's Crispy Duck

with coconut salad

SERVES 1

1 duck leg

Master stock
2L chicken stock
½ cup Shoaxing wine
½ cup sweet soy sauce
100g rock sugar
2 whole shallots
1 medium knob ginger, sliced
3 star anise
1 piece cassia bark

Tamarind dressing
200ml tamarind water
50g palm sugar
20ml fish sauce
50ml lime juice
sm pinch chilli powder

Salad
15 sprigs coriander leaves, picked with stem on
6 medium mint leaves
40g shaved coconut
50g bean sprouts
4 cherry tomatoes, halved
½ red chilli, julienned
½ eshalot, sliced
2 kaffir lime leaves, julienned
8g peanuts
4g eshalots, deep-fried

For master stock, place all ingredients in a pot, bring to the boil and let simmer. Add duck leg and cook for 20 minutes. Let duck leg cool down in the stock then refrigerate overnight. The following day take the leg out of the master stock.

For the dressing, dissolve the palm sugar with the fish sauce in a mortar and pestle. Add tamarind water, lime juice and chilli powder and mix. The dressing should taste sweet, salty and sour.

Deep-fry duck leg till golden brown then cool and shred.

Mix in a bowl together with the salad ingredients, adding 20-50ml of dressing and tossing well. Can be served in a bowl or on a flat plate.

Belinda Jeffery's

Warm Figs with Honey, Mandarin and Cinnamon

SERVES 4

8 - 10 medium ripe figs
50g unsalted butter
¼ cup clear honey
1 tbs finely grated mandarin (or orange) zest
1½ - 2 tbs freshly squeezed mandarin (or orange) juice
½ tsp ground cinnamon , good quality vanilla ice cream; or a mixture of equal parts lightly-sweetened, softly whipped cream and thick Greek-style plain yoghurt, to serve
toasted flaked almonds, optional

Preheat oven to 200°C.

Halve the figs lengthways (although you can keep really tiny ones whole) and nestle them snugly, cut-side up, in a shallow glass or ceramic oven-proof dish (a gratin dish is ideal).

Put the butter, honey, mandarin zest, mandarin juice, and cinnamon into a small saucepan over low-ish heat. Stir the mixture until the butter melts and the honey dissolves, then remove the pan from the heat and drizzle the mixture evenly over the figs.

Place dish in the oven and cook the figs for 15 minutes or until they're very tender but not turning to mush. When they're ready, sit the dish on a trivet or rack and let the figs cool a little.

Serve while they're warm, dividing them equally between serving bowls and drizzling the buttery juices over the top. Add a dollop of the yoghurt mixture or a scoop of ice-cold ice cream (my favorite, as I love the way the warm fig juices mingle with the melting ice cream to form a luscious 'sauce'). If you like, scatter some almonds on top to add a toasty, nutty crunch.

an early walk to the lighthouse — a must

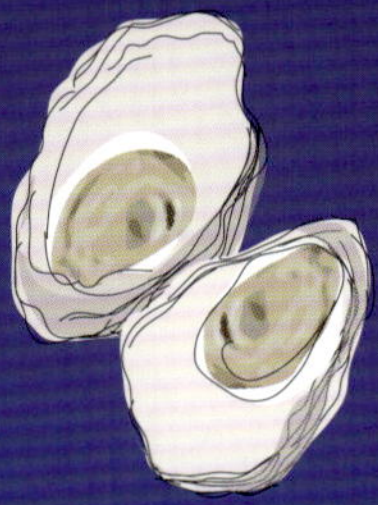

Heading North

As you head north from Byron Bay the countryside is mesmerising – undulating hills, lush green landscapes, farm houses, banana plantations, and of course rivers. All the while, looking over your shoulder are the menacing peaks, firstly of Mount Chincogan in Mullumbimby, and then Mount Warning near Murwillumbah.

You'll pass through several smaller, older towns along the way and by the time you arrive up in the stunning new beach-side settlements of Cabarita, Casaurina, Kingscliff and Salt Village, you'll be ready to book a room, have a dip in the ocean and enjoy the village atmosphere.

From the historic holiday town of Kingscliff, head inland and find the big old regional lady that is Murwillumbah on the Tweed River – famous for the regional art gallery, and large farming population. It's a perfect place to end this first leg of your journey.

Bayleaf's Sausage and Eggs

with salsa verde

SERVES 1

1 Hayters Hill Italian sausage
3 Hayters Hill free-range eggs
½ habanero chilli, sliced finely
1 tbs each sliced green onions and torn parsley
1 slice good quality sourdough

Salsa verde

1 cup flat-leaf parsley leaves
1 cup basil leaves
1 garlic clove, chopped
2 tsp capers, drained
½ cup extra-virgin olive oil
1 lemon, juiced
sea salt

Grill or fry the Italian sausage. Crack eggs into a bowl and whisk until combined (add a dash of cream if you like). Add chilli, green onions and parsley to egg mix.

Once sausage is just about cooked, toast sourdough and place pan on heat to prepare for the scrambled eggs. Add a dash of oil to a pan and when hot add eggs, chilli and sliced green onion and cook to your liking.

Prepare the salsa verde by placing the parsley, basil, garlic and capers in a food processor and process until finely chopped. With the motor running slowly add the oil and lemon juice to the mixture. This can be kept in the fridge for a week.

Lay eggs on toast, place sausage on top and spoon over 2 tablespoons of the salsa verde.

Bayleaf's Smoked Chicken

and charred pepper salad

SERVES 2

150-200g smoked chicken
1 cup of cooked buckwheat, or other grain
1 charred green/red pepper, deseeded and sliced lengthwise
½ avocado, flesh scooped out of skin
100g cherry tomatoes, halved
1 tbs toasted sunflower/pumpkin seeds
handful of leaves (rocket, lettuce, cress, herbs)

Dressing

good quality white wine vinegar
good quality olive oil
zest and juice of 1 lemon
salt and pepper to taste

Slice smoked chicken.

To make the dressing, combine all ingredients in a jar and shake.

Add all ingredients to a bowl in the following order: avocado, peppers, tomatoes, chicken, buckwheat, seeds, leaves and herbs.

Toss through dressing to combine well and serve.

Byron Beach Cafe's

Seared Mahi-mahi with Chorizo, Rancho Mixed Bean Salsa, Wilted Spinach and Balmain Bugs

SERVES 4

4 180g Mahi-mahi fillets, skin off
2 whole fresh Balmain Bugs
200g chorizo sausage
100ml olive oil
1kg fresh spinach
2 large lemons
1 punnet baby micro herbs

Rancho Mixed Bean Salsa

200g dried cannelloni beans
50g rinsed salted black beans
1 large red capsicum seeded and diced into large pieces
1 large green capsicum seeded and diced into large pieces
2 garlic cloves peeled and finely sliced
1 large brown onion peeled and diced
1 large red chilli finely sliced
200g peeled crushed tomatoes
1 tsp smoked paprika
1 tsp ground cumin
salt and pepper to taste
¼ tsp chilli powder

To make the rancho mixed bean salsa, soak the cannelloni beans overnight in cold water.

Using a colander, wash the salted black beans under running water until the water runs clear.

Simmer the cannelloni beans in a small saucepan on low heat until tender, strain and refrigerate until chilled.

Heat a tablespoon of olive oil in a large frying pan, sauté the brown onion, garlic and chilli until soft but not coloured. Add the smoked paprika, cumin and chilli powder. Mix well and cook for 2 minutes on a low heat.

Add the capsicums and cook for 5 minutes, stirring to combine all ingredients.

Add the crushed tomatoes and continue cooking until capsicum has softened.

Season with salt and pepper and set aside to rest.

In a fresh frying pan, heat a tablespoon of olive oil and sauté the diced chorizo on high heat for 5 minutes. Add the cooked cannelloni beans, rinsed salted black beans and the rancho sauce mix. Combine all ingredients, reduce the heat and simmer for 20 minutes.

To prepare the Balmain Bugs and Mahi-mahi, first preheat the oven to 180°C.

Wash the Mahi-mahi fillets and Balmain Bugs and pat dry with kitchen paper.

Place the whole Balmain Bugs on a chopping board and using a sharp knife cut in half from top to bottom and devein.

Season the Mahi-mahi fillets with salt and pepper.

In a large smoking hot pan saute the Mahi-mahi fillets with a tablespoon of olive oil (you may want to turn on your extractor fan for this). Cook Mahi-mahi fillets until golden brown, then turn and repeat on the other side (approximately 2 minutes each side).

Add half a Balmain Bug, meat side down to the pan, with the Mahi-mahi fillets and quickly seal (approximately 30 seconds).

Place the Mahi-mahi fillets and the Balmain Bugs on a baking tray and place in the oven at 180°C for 6 minutes or until the Mahi-mahi fillets are cooked through.

In a fresh frying pan, sauté spinach on low heat in a little olive oil and season with salt and pepper.

To serve place two large spoonfuls of the rancho mixed bean salsa in the centre of the plate, top with a spoonful of wilted spinach, a cooked Mahi-mahi fillet and a Balmain Bug, garnish with micro herbs, a splash of olive oil and a wedge of lemon. Serve immediately.

Preparare la crema con
un etto di zucchero, e un quarto di litro abbondante
di latte e profumo di vaniglia, facendo
attenzione di ritirarla appena accenna
a bollire, e aggiungervi subito tre fogli
di colla di pesce già messa a bagno dieci
minuti prima.
Lasciarla freddare mescolando ogni
tanto, e quando comincerà a rapprendersi
unirvi con delicatezza la panna montata.
Versarla in uno stampo appena unto
d'olio fine, e mettere in acqua ben
fresca o meglio sul ghiaccio per due ore.

The Pass Café's

Warm Lamb Salad

SERVES 4

600g lamb backstrap or rump
3 cloves garlic, crushed
4 sprigs fresh rosemary, leaves
½ cup olive oil
salt and pepper to taste

Salad

8 whole fresh baby beetroot
2 large red capsicums
500g mesclun
250g feta
1 large red onion

Tatziki

1 cup Greek yoghurt
12 mint leaves, finely sliced
½ cup continental cucumber, de-seeded and grated
juice ½ lemon

Salad dressing

½ cup olive oil
1 tbs balsamic vinegar
1 tbs red wine vinegar

Combine lamb, olive oil and crushed garlic in a large bowl and marinate for 3 hours prior or preferably overnight. Coat capsicums in olive oil and roast in 180°C oven until soft and outside skin is charred.

Peel and quarter baby beetroot then place in oven and roast until cooked, approximately 20 minutes. Dice feta into 1cm cubes and thinly slice red onion. Thoroughly wash and drain the mesclun.

For tatziki, combine mint leaves, yoghurt, lemon juice and cucumber in a bowl and set to one side.

For the dressing, combine all the ingredients and shake in a jar until combined. Place in the fridge.

Once capsicum is cooked, peel, de-seed and cut into generous size pieces.

Add a splash of olive oil to a frypan and place the lamb in pan. Seal all sides then place in a preheated oven at 220°C for approximately 5 minutes or until lamb feels like it has just a little bit of give to it. For well-done lamb extend the cooking time. Once cooked, remove from the oven and set to one side to rest for approximately 2 to 5 minutes. Combine salad ingredients in a large bowl and mix thoroughly then add salad dressing to taste.

To serve, place a generous handful of salad in the middle of a large bowl. Slice lamb thinly and place 4 or 5 slices on top of the salad. Using a tablespoon place a large dollop of tatziki on top of the lamb. Decorate with a balsamic glaze if available and serve.

Guy Skinner- Hutchison's

Rae's Moreton Bay Bug Ravioli Tomato Saffron Bisque Char-grilled Bug

SERVES 4

Pasta

300g plain flour
3 eggs
1 tsp salt

Ravioli stuffing

2 whole green bugs halved
200g diced bug meat
6 whole green prawns peel and keep shells, diced into cubes
80g ocean trout or salmon
zest of 2 lemons
chervil / parsley, half a bunch of each
seasoning salt
40 ml cream

Bisque

6 prawn shells
3 tbs tomato paste
40ml extra virgin olive oil

Bug sauce

2 large carrots
6 large eshallots
2 celery sticks peeled
4 cloves garlic
2 x 500g whole peeled tinned tomatoes (remove core) keep juice and flesh
1g saffron
2 ltr prawn stock / bisque
80ml Vermouth, Pernod or white wine

To serve

seasonal green vegetables
herbs
extra virgin olive oil
capsicum seeded and diced into large pieces
2 garlic cloves finely sliced
1 large brown onion diced
1 large red chilli finely sliced
200g peeled crushed tomatoes
1 tsp smoked paprika
1 tsp ground cumin
salt and pepper to taste
¼ teaspoon chilli powder

To make pasta, pulse in food processor until combined then turn out to the bench and knead for five minutes until smooth. Allow to rest for 10-15 minutes. Roll pasta, setting to 3 (depending on your machine) and cut desired shape. Use an egg yolk to seal the ravioli. Chef note - use your finger to apply the yolk but only just a little bit as too much and it will not stick at all.

To make ravioli stuffing, dice bug and prawns and place in a mixing bowl. Add chopped herbs and using a microplane zest your lemons. Place the fish in the food processor, mix until fish is mousse consistency, add your cream and season. Combine your fish mousse, bug and prawn mix. Test a little piece in a fry pan for seasoning. Shape into 40g to 60g balls.

To make bisque, heat a large heavy based saucepan. Place prawn shells and a generous splash of extra virgin olive oil in the pot. Cook for 5 to 8 minutes till prawn shells have turned a beautiful orange colour. Add tomato paste and mix well so all prawn shells are coated; be sure to cook out the tomato paste for 10 minutes on a low heat. Chef note: if the pot is looking a little dry use some more olive oil.

Now your prawns are smelling amazing add 2/3 litre of filtered water and allow to simmer on a low heat for a minimum 1 hour. Strain through muslin or a fine sieve.

To make bug sauce, dice small to medium (see photo) carrot, eshallot, celery, slice garlic. Heat a large base saucepan add a splash of cooking oil add your diced vegies.

Sauté on a medium heat for 5 minutes add your saffron and then deglaze, (pour your Vermouth, white wine or Pernod into the hot pot), allow to evaporate till the smallest amount of liquid is left then add your amazing prawn stock and tomatoes.

Reduce for 15 minutes on a low heat. Once the sauce has had time to sit (10 or 15 minutes is fine), taste and adjust seasoning.

Once the half shell bug is on the pan and or in the oven, place ravioli in the boiling water and allow 3 to 5 minutes cooking time. Place sauce back on the high heat stirring occasionally.

Place vegetables in water with the ravioli. Remove from water and drain. Dress with olive oil, salt and lemon juice. Now we are ready to plate!

Remove bug from pan and place on the plate, place the ravioli and vegies on the plate and then very gently ladle your saffron tomato bisque over the ravioli. Garnish with herbs and olive oil.

Victoria's Smoked Salmon Souffle Roulade

with caviar

SERVES 6

½ cup unsalted butter
½ cup plain flour
½ tsp cayenne pepper
½ tsp salt
1½ cups milk
12 eggs, separated
½ tsp cream of tartar
500g smoked salmon
200g cream cheese
½ cup chopped dill
20g salmon caviar

Preheat oven to 200°C. Grease and line a baking dish with baking paper. In a pot over low heat, melt the butter, then whisk in flour, cayenne pepper and salt and cook for 3 minutes. Add milk, whisk until smooth then let cool. Beat eggs yolks and add to the cooled flour mix.

In a separate bowl beat egg whites and cream of tartar together until stiff peaks form then gently fold into the egg yolk mix. Pour mix into the lined baking dish and bake in the oven for 15 minutes or until it springs back when touched. Turn out and cool.

Mix cream cheese and dill together, spread over the cooled soufflé then layer smoked salmon over the top. Roll into a roulade, wrap in foil and refrigerate. When ready to serve, heat the roulade in a moderate oven for 3 minutes, then cut into slices and serve with salmon caviar.

Belongil Bistro's Pan-fried Potato Gnocchi

with duck, peas, speck and thyme

SERVES 4

Gnocchi

1kg large desiree potatoes
1 cup table salt or sea salt for baking
1 whole egg
50g finely grated parmesan
150g plain flour (plus extra for dusting)
½ tsp table salt

Duck confit

4 duck legs
50g sea salt
1ltr canola oil (a couple of spoons of duck fat also if you can get it)
8 sprigs thyme
6 black peppercorns
1 bay leaf

Pea puree

300g frozen peas
200ml boiling chicken stock
1 pinch salt

For the dish

800g potato gnocchi
50ml canola oil for frying
4 duck confit, flaked
100g whole peas
400g pea puree
8 thin slices speck or pancetta
100g shaved parmesan
½ bunch watercress

For the potato gnocchi, make a thin bed of the salt on a baking tray and place the potatoes on it. Bake at 170°C for 1 hour 15 minutes or until you can get a knife in them and they feel soft like butter. The cooking time will vary depending on the size of the potatoes. When they come out of the oven you have to work quickly to prevent them from going cold. If they do the recipe won't work well enough.

Meanwhile, prepare a medium pan of boiling water. Have a bowl filled with cold water and a few ice cubes in it plus a small sieve or slotted spoon handy.

Let the potatoes cool for 5 minutes, then, wearing a pair of rubber gloves so you don't burn yourself, cut them in half and scoop the fluffy hot insides into a large flour sieve, pushing the potatoes through with the back of a large spoon as you go. You should end up with a small pile of steaming dry mashed potato on your work surface.

Now quickly push your fingers in it to spread it out and make holes in it. Scatter the parmesan on it which you want to warm so it binds with the potato properly. Crack the egg on to it next, followed by the salt and plain flour.

Bring the whole lot together with your hands and begin to knead to form a sticky dough, sprinkling on some of the excess flour to prevent it sticking to the work surface or your hands.

Cut the ball into 4 and roll each one into thin sausages, flouring the bench lightly as you go. Cut them into little pillows by simply pushing through with a straight edge such as a blunt knife or scraper. Scoop them towards you and onto a plate then repeat with the remaining 3 balls.

Empty a plate at a time into the boiling water and lift them out with the spoon or sieve when they bob to the surface, dropping them into the iced water to cool them quickly.

When they are all cooked and cooled, drain them in a colander, drizzle with a little olive oil and gently toss to prevent them sticking together. Pour them onto a large plate or tray so they aren't sitting on top of each other and refrigerate, uncovered. Now clean up and get ready for the next stage which can be between 1 and 6 hours later. If left overnight cover them with cling-wrap for up to 3 days.

To make the duck confit, rub the duck legs with the sea salt and lay on paper towel on a plate. Refrigerate overnight to draw water out.

Rinse off with cold water and soak in fresh water for 1 hour. Lift out, pat dry and lay in a baking tin.

Submerge in remaining ingredients, cover with foil and bake at 140°C for 3 hours. Remove from the oven and leave to cool in the oil. When room temperature, lift out and flake the meat off the bone. By all means tear up the skin and put it through the meat for a bit of extra luxury. The skin will crisp up when you fry it.

Throw the oil in the garden bed or strain and freeze for the next time you confit some duck legs.

Make a pea puree by putting the peas in a blender, add a pinch of salt, pour over the hot stock and puree. Scoop into a microwave-proof bowl and cover in cling-wrap.

In a large non-stick frying pan heat a teaspoon of oil. Place the slices of speck or pancetta in oil and turn the heat down. Gently fry until crispy, just like cooking crispy bacon. Lay on paper towel to crisp up.

Without cleaning the pan heat it again and pour in the remaining oil. Gently lower in half the gnocchi and half the flaked duck meat, frying until golden. If the pan isn't hot enough they won't get crispy and golden on the outside; if they spend too long in the pan they will soften and break down, losing their beautiful shape and sticking together. Empty into a stainless steel mixing bowl then repeat the process with the remaining gnocchi and duck.

When all is cooked toss the gnocchi with the whole peas and place in a hot oven for a few minutes to keep warm.

Heat the pea puree in the microwave and either pour over the gnocchi and toss through or present on the plate in some way.

Spoon the gnocchi onto the plates and garnish with the crispy speck, shaved parmesan and watercress. Serve with a nice glass of pinot noir or blood orange juice for the kids.

belongilbistro.com.au

Brookfarm's Muesli Hedgehog Slice

with cranberries and pistachios

SERVES 16

¼ cup coconut cream
200g dark chocolate (45% cocoa solids), chopped roughly
2 cups Brookfarm Cranberry Macadamia Gluten Free Muesli
½ cup desiccated coconut, plus 2 tbs extra
¼ cup shelled salted pistachios
extra pistachios, cranberries and macadamias to top

Line a square 20cm slice tin with baking paper.

Place the coconut cream in a small saucepan and heat over low heat until it comes to a simmer. Remove from the heat and add chopped chocolate. Stir until the chocolate is glossy and melted.

Place the muesli, ½ cup desiccated coconut and pistachios in a large bowl and mix well. Add half of the melted chocolate and stir to combine. Spoon mixture over base of tin, (pressing gently into corners).

Add the extra 2 tablespoons desiccated coconut to the remaining melted chocolate and mix. Pour over the slice and spread evenly. Top with extra pistachios, cranberries and macadamias.

Refrigerate overnight or until firm then turn on to a board and cut into 16 squares.

Brookfarm's Scallops with Shaved Fennel

in a lemon myrtle vinaigrette

SERVES 4

16 scallops – roe removed (can leave on if you're a roe lover)
1 knob fennel finely shaved
1 tbs finely chopped fennel leaves
1 heaped teaspoon Dijon mustard (no seeds)
¼ cup white balsamic vinegar
¼ cup Brookfarm Lemon Myrtle infused Macadamia Oil
¼ cup Brookfarm Premium Grade natural Macadamia Oil
salt and pepper to taste
1 tbs butter
¼ cup Brookfarm Premium Grade natural Macadamia Oil
salt and pepper to taste
edible flowers to decorate

Put finely sliced fennel and chopped leaves in a bowl.

In a separate cup add Lemon Myrtle Macadamia Oil, Natural Macadamia Oil, white balsamic vinegar and Dijon mustard, add salt and pepper to taste, shake vigorously until a smooth even mix and pour over sliced fennel, season to taste.

Lightly season scallops with salt and pepper.

Heat heavy frypan to high heat and add macadamia oil and butter, then add the scallops and sear to a light brown on each side (approximately 1 min per side) so just cooked through.

Place scallops on to shells and add a drizzle of the brown butter/macadamia oil from the pan.

Place the dressed shaved fennel over the scallop, decorate with an edible flower and serve.

Brookfarm's Fried Green Tomatoes

in brown ale beer batter with macadamia salsa

SERVES 4

200ml Brookfarm Premium Grade Natural Macadamia Oil
3 green heritage tomatoes (we use Coopers Shoot tomatoes)
1½ cups self-raising flour
1 bottle (330ml) chilled Stone and Wood Pacific Ale or similar rich brown ale
½ tsp salt
cracked black pepper to taste

Macadamia salsa

125g Brookfarm Oven Roasted macadamias coarsely chopped (if unavailable gently dry-roast raw macadamias in oven at 125°C for 10-15 minutes – watch closely so they don't over-brown)
1 cup coarsely chopped coriander
1 tbs honey
1 tsp balsamic vinegar
1 seeded finely chopped red chilli

Place flour, salt and pepper in mixing bowl and gently add beer while whisking with fork.

Blend thoroughly to remove all lumps. Batter should be thick and smooth. Put batter aside in the fridge to chill.

Cut tomatoes into slices (not to thin, not too thick, about 0.75cm), then place tomatoes on paper towel to remove excess moisture.

Heat about half the macadamia oil in large heavy-based fry pan, oil should be about 1 cm deep, with the heat to medium/high. Test if ready by adding a drop of batter, the oil should bubble around it and batter should rise to surface.

Dip tomato slices gently in the batter and place in the frypan.

Cook on high heat for 2-3 minutes or until browned on one side, turn with tongs and brown on the other side.

Remove from pan and place on paper towel to remove any excess oil.

Coarsely chop roasted macadamias in food processor or by hand, add coriander and chilli and stir through honey and balsamic vinegar.

Season to taste with salt and pepper.

To serve, top each fried tomato with 1 heaped teaspoon salsa.

Serve immediately while hot and don't forget to drink any left over beer!

Stone & Wood's

Chocolate Espresso Cupcakes

MAKES 18

Cupcake Batter

1 cup Stone and Wood Stone Beer
280g unsalted butter
¾ cup sifted unsweetened cocoa
1 cup soft brown sugar
1 cup caster sugar
¾ cup sour cream
2 large eggs
1 tbs vanilla essence
2 cups sifted plain flour
2 1/2 tsp baking soda

Chocolate Stone Beer Ganache

(The ganache is piped inside the cupcake before cooking for a luscious soft centre)
220g good quality dark chocolate
125ml coconut cream
100ml Stone and Wood Stone Beer
25g glucose
2 tbs cream
50gm butter cubed

Expresso Buttercream Icing

200g very soft unsalted butter
450g sifted icing sugar
2 tbs milk
½ tsp vanilla extract
50 - 100ml cold expresso coffee add to taste and consistency
12 Byron Bay dark chocolate coffee beans, to decorate

Heat the oven to 175°C. Place your cupcake cases ready on a tray.

In a saucepan, combine beer and butter, cook over medium heat until the butter melts, then remove from heat, add sifted cocoa, caster sugar and brown sugar, whisk to blend.

In a bowl, combine sour cream, eggs and vanilla essence, mix well.

Add to beer mix, whisk well. Add sifted flour and baking soda, whisk again until smooth.

Prepare 2 piping bags; fill one bag with the cupcake batter and the other with the chocolate ganache. Pipe the batter into the cupcake cases only filling halfway, and then pipe a decent amount of the ganache mixture into the middle of each cupcake. Finish with the batter mix again, taking care not to overfill.

Bake in a preheated oven at 175°C for approximately 25 minutes, or until cupcakes spring back. They should be a bit gooey. Cool on a rack.

Once cooled decorate with espresso buttercream icing and a coffee bean.

To make the chocolate Stone Beer ganache (this can be prepared before the cupcake batter and set aside), place the dark chocolate in a bowl. Put the coconut milk, Stone Beer, glucose and cream in a saucepan, bring to the boil over a medium heat.

Pour the boiling mix over the chocolate. Let it sit for 20 seconds. Then whisk it all together until the chocolate is melted. Whisk in the butter until the mixture is very smooth. Set aside to cool for a short time. Stir well before using.

To make the espresso buttercream icing, whisk butter well and till very pale, add sifted icing sugar, adding half at a time. Whisk very well. It will be very pale.

Add milk and vanilla extract. Add cooled espresso coffee in a slow stream down the side of the bowl. Add to taste and consistency, and colour. You should be able to taste the coffee.

To decorate the cupcakes, place icing in a spoon, plop, turn, bounce and flourish on top.

Place a coffee bean on the top of each cupcake to serve. Chill or even better, serve fresh.

Note: Stone Beer exhibits dark fruits, toasted nuts and sweet caramel flavours

Top Shop's Chocolate Brioche

SERVES 12

1 tbs raw sugar
2 cups plain flour
3 eggs, whisked
125g salted butter, roughly chopped
1 cup of good quality dark chocolate buttons
7g sachet of dried yeast
¼ cup warm full-cream milk
¼ cup caster sugar

Mix together the milk, half the caster sugar and yeast in bowl. Cover with a tea towel and set aside in a warm place for 10 minutes. Mix together the rest of the caster sugar and flour in a bowl, adding a pinch of salt. Add the three whisked eggs and the yeast mixture and gently fold together with a wooden spoon until a sticky dough forms. Tip the dough out on to a well- floured work-bench and knead, adding the chopped butter and chocolate buttons as you go. Continue kneading until it becomes silky-smooth. Put the dough into a greased bowl, cover and leave to rise. It should double in size over about 45 minutes.

Line a muffin tray with individual grease-paper cups, or, if preferred, you can just grease the moulds. Remove the dough from the bowl and knead again on work-bench for a minute or so. Divide the dough into eight and roll each portion into a ball. Place each ball, with the smoothest side facing up, into the muffin moulds.

Allow the buns to rise in a warm place for about 45 minutes. Apply an egg wash evenly, and then bake for 15 to 20 minutes at 180°C. Serve with poached pears and a dollop of yogurt or double cream.

Top Shop's Braised Portobello Mushrooms

SERVES 4

16 lge Portobello mushrooms
4 cloves garlic, crushed
1½ cups white wine
200g salted butter
8 sprigs thyme
½ cup olive oil
½ cup lemon juice
1 cup chopped parsley
sea salt flakes and pepper

In a large deep baking tray, lay out the mushrooms with the underside facing up, slightly overlapping. Pour over the wine then liberally season with cracked pepper and seasalt flakes.

Dot around the garlic and butter evenly, then pour over the olive oil. Strip half the thyme sprigs and scatter over the leaves evenly, then toss the other 4 sprigs on top. Cover the tray with foil and place in the oven at 180°C for an hour.

Remove from the oven, take off the foil then return to the oven and bake for another half hour, or until most the liquid has evaporated and the mushrooms are a deep rich colour and quite dry. Place in a bowl, add the chopped parsley and lemon juice and dash of olive oil. Combine then cover for 10 minutes.

Serve on hot buttered sourdough, with a wedge of lemon.

~TOP SHOP~
~Farms & Suppliers~
Hayters Hill Farm - eggs+beef
Alstonville Poultry Farm-chicken
Witches Broomstick-mushies
Bangalow Sweet Pork-bacon
Meads Butcher - salumi
Glenbrook Farm-figs+berrie
Craig's Banana Farm
Bay Seafood - whiting
Fundies-organic flour
Barambah Dairy-milk
Coopers Shoot Tomatoes
Jordans Organic Bakery
From The Bay BBQ sauce
Tiers+Treats cakes
Single origin Roasters
VINCE JONES
AFRICA
BURGERS
COFFEE
ANDWICHES

Victoria's Petit Chocolate Cheesecake Tarts

with fresh berries

MAKES 9 TARTS

Chocolate pastry

200g plain flour
50g cocoa powder
2 tbs icing sugar
200g cold butter, cubed
160ml sour cream

Filling

250g cream cheese
¾ cup caster sugar
1 tbs gelatine
½ cup boiling water
300ml cream
strawberries, raspberries, blueberries

For the pastry, sift flour, cocoa and icing sugar together. Place into a food processor and add the butter and combine until the mixture resembles breadcrumbs. Add the sour cream and pulse until combined. Tip onto a lightly floured work surface and knead to combine.

Cover with cling-film and refrigerate for 20 minutes. Roll out the pastry and cut to fit into small tart tins. Blind-bake at 180°C for 5 minutes or until cooked.

For the filling, mix together cream cheese and sugar. Dissolve gelatine in boiling water then add to the cream cheese mix. Whip the cream then fold into the cream cheese mix when cooled.

Fill the tart cases with the filling and set in the fridge for 6 hours. Top the tarts with fresh berries and serve.

Darren Robertson and Mark LaBrooy's

Charred Prawns with Chilli and Confit Garlic

SERVES 4

1 bulb garlic, peeled
5 long red chillies, deseeded and roughly chopped
200ml olive oil
2 tbs vegetable oil
16 lge green prawns, shell and heads on, butterflied and cleaned
1 1/2 lemons, zest and juice kept separately
1/4 bunch continental parsley, finely chopped
Salt and pepper

Preheat the oven to 160°C.

Take a small saucepan with a steel handle that can be put in the oven. Place the garlic, chilli and olive oil, along with plenty of cracked pepper into the saucepan, cover the saucepan with foil and put it in the oven for 1½ hours.

Once cooled, pour the contents of the saucepan into your food processor and blitz until a chilli and garlic paste forms.

Divide the paste in half and add the chopped parsley to one half. Brush the flesh side of the butterfly prawns with the parsley and garlic mix and season well.

Turn your BBQ on both the chargrill and the flat-top side. Chargrill the butterfly prawns flesh side down for a couple of minutes, and then flip them over. This process will only take a few minutes, be careful not to overcook the prawns.

Once cooked, take the prawns off the BBQ and sprinkle with the zest and juice of the lemons.

Serve with a fresh garden salad, like kale, spinach or a citrus radish herb salad tossed in olive oil.

Fig Tree's

Ponzu Cured Flame Tail Snapper

SERVES 20 AS A TASTER

Ponzu

400ml light soy
400ml citrus juice (orange, lemon and lime)
200ml mirin
1 clove garlic
20g peeled ginger

Beetroot cured kingfish

1.5 kg kingfish
2 large beetroot grated
zest and juice from 2 oranges
½ bunch dill
½ bunch chive
100ml gin
1g salt
2g sugar
1.5 kg flame tail snapper

Labne

500g of natural yoghurt
1 tbs lemon zest

Spiced crumb

500g of seeded rice and tapioca bread (diced)
5g ground cumin, pepper and fennel seed

To make the Ponzu, blend all ingredients in a food processor until well combined, strain before serving.

For the cured kingfish, combine all aromatics and gin with salt and sugar and cover kingfish in deep tray. Press for 24 hours.

Thinly slice to order. Be sure to wash off marinade before serving

To make the labne, mix 500g of natural yoghurt with lemon zest and hang in a strainer lined with cheese cloth overnight.

To make the spiced crumb, dice seeded rice and tapioca bread and mix with 5g cumin, pepper and fennel seed. Toast all ingredients in a low oven for 2 hours. Blitz in food processor until it forms a fine crumb

To prepare the snapper, thinly slice and dress with the Ponzu to serve.

Fig Tree's

Bangalow Sweet Pork Neck, Pork Belly Confit with Pear and Muscatels

SERVES 20

Braised pork neck

1kg of trimmed pork neck
5 cloves of minced garlic
1/2 a bunch of thyme
1 tsp of sweet smoked paprika
1/2 red onion, diced
2 ltr basic brown vegetable stock
1 tsp toasted, ground fennel seed

Pear purée

500g peeled, cored and diced pear
cinnamon and clove-infused sugar syrup
20 small muscatels (soak dried muscatels in peppermint tea overnight and pick into individual grapes)

Pork belly confit

1 pork belly (approx. 3 kg), bone out
100g sea salt
2 ltr pure duck fat

Dice pork neck into large chunks.

Roast on high heat in deep oven tray until pork starts to brown. Add prepared vegetables and spices and roast for a further 5 minutes. Cover with vegetable stock and seal tray with foil.

Braise for 2 hours on low heat. Once cooked, remove braising liquid by 3/4 and then add back to pork.

Once completed, roll pork into a tight cylinder using cling film and allow to cool overnight in fridge before slicing.

Combine pear, sugar and muscatels and bring to boil. Boil for 10 minutes, then remove from heat and allow to cool.

Remove pear from syrup and puree until smooth.

Salt pork belly for at least 1 hour.

Remove excess salt and submerge in duck fat.

Confite in deep oven tray at 160°C for 3 hours.

Remove from duck fat and press under weight overnight.

Cut into 50g squares and roast on high just before serving.

Fig Tree's

Goat Cheese Pannacotta with Fig and Black Rice Snap

SERVES 4-6

Pannacotta

700ml full cream milk
300g goats curd
¼ bunch thyme
1 sprig rosemary
¼ bunch sage
20g black peppercorns
½ brown onion
10g salt (to taste)
3 sheets gelatine
3 bay leaves
2 figs
200g honeycomb

Black rice snap

300g "gluteness" black rice
salt to taste

Sauce

5 Figs
1 cup of red wine
3 tbs of sugar
1 cinnamon quill
1 star anise

Gently infuse aromatic herbs into milk careful not to boil. Bloom gelatine in water. Strain all ingredients from milk while still hot. Blend infused milk with goats curd and gelatine until smooth. Set in 50ml moulds and allow to cool overnight.

Boil black rice over high heat until cooked. Season with salt to taste. Spread 4mm thick onto tray lined with grease proof paper. Dehydrate for 24 hours or until crispy. Snap into shards and gently deep fry to serve.

For the sauce, slice and grill figs for 3-5 minutes. Combine red wine with sugar, cinnamon and star anise and bring to boil, pour over figs. Leave to cool. Serve cold.

To serve, slice figs and place on plate with honeycomb.

Bluesfest

Oysters

Enjoy fresh oysters natural with a squeeze of lemon... and really the one-and-only way we eat oysters is with tomato sauce and horseradish!

JR's Smokehouse Barbecue

Slow Smoked Barbecue Ribs with Texas-style BBQ Sauce

SERVES 2

2-3 racks of non-marinated pork ribs (USA cut). Each rack should weigh at least 1kg

The rub

1 cup brown sugar
¼ cup paprika
2 tbs kosher salt
2 tbs ground black pepper
1 tbs chilli powder
2 tbs garlic powder
2 tbs onion powder
½ tsp cayenne pepper for heat
mustard to rub

Texas-style BBQ sauce

½ cup unsalted butter
½ onion, finely chopped
2 cups (bottled) tomato sauce
¾ cup cider vinegar
¼ cup brown sugar
1 tsp Kosher salt
1 tbs black pepper
1 tsp chilli powder
¼ cup lemon juice

For the rub, combine all ingredients. Rub top side of ribs with light coat of mustard then sprinkle a light coat of rub on both sides. Cover in cling-film and refrigerate for several hours or dust them right before they go on.

For the sauce, melt butter in a saucepan and add the onion then all the other ingredients. Simmer for 15 minutes, stirring frequently.

Light fire and heat to 120°C. Once fire is steady, put the ribs on, bone-side down. Maintain temperature at 120°C for the 5-6 hour duration of the cooking, using an oven thermometer if necessary. Add a few wood chunks to the coals and close the lid, resisting the urge to keep looking at the meat. After 3 hours remove the ribs from the pit. Spritz with apple juice and wrap tightly in aluminum foil for 90 minutes. After 4½ hours remove, coat with sauce and return to grill for final 30-60 minutes. If they still feel firm keep cooking until meat is able to be shredded or 'pulled' easily. Let them rest for 15 minutes then cut in two's and three's. Serve with traditional Southern sides such as coleslaw, potato salad and ranch beans.

What you need

A wood-fired smoker or common Weber kettle barbecue with lid. (If using the latter set it up for indirect cooking by lighting coals on one side and no coals on the other side: you will cook the ribs on the side opposite the fire.) You'll also need wood charcoal (for heat) and seasoned hardwood (for flavour).

Kingscliff Beach Hotel's

Sticky Crispy Pork Belly Salad

with fish caramel and chilli cucumber

SERVES 4-6

Pork belly

2kg pork belly (approx. ½ belly)
500ml orchard crush apple cider
½ cup salt (rubbing)
Mirepoix* of carrot, onion, celery

Fish caramel

400g caster sugar
400ml water
50ml fish sauce

Salad

2 continental cucumbers (rolling cut)
1 spanish onion (thinly sliced)
2 tbs chilli sambal (to taste)
bean sprouts
picked mint leaves

Salt the pork belly and place on top of mirepoix in roasting tray. Pour cider down side. Place in a pre-heated oven. Cook on 140°C for 2.5 hours, then 200°C for 20-30 minutes until skin has crackled.

Allow to cool, take belly out of tray, scrape off excess salt, and cut into thick 2cm diced.

Combine sugar, water and fish sauce on low heat, reduce to a caramel.

Fry cubed belly in a pan until hot, toss through caramel sauce, lay out onto long serving plate, drizzle with left over caramel.

Toss cucumber, onion, mint leaves and chilli in a bowl, lay over top of pork, finish with bean sprouts and mint leaves.

*Mirepoix is a flavouring made from diced vegetables, placed in a pan to cook with fish or meat.

Mockingbird Cafe's

Beetroot-Cured Salmon with Cornbread

SERVES 4

Salmon

1 side (approx 2kg) pin-boned and skin-off salmon
400g cooked, pureed beetroot
4 cups coarse sea salt
4 cups caster sugar
20 juniper berries
zest of 1 large lemon

Cornbread

1 cup gluten-free flour
4 tsp baking powder
1 tsp salt
170g cornmeal (polenta)
60g caster sugar
60ml olive oil
1 egg
½ cup soy milk
1 x 400g tin creamed corn
1 cup fresh corn, cut from the cob
¼ cup fresh thyme
¼ cup fresh sage, finely sliced
extra sage and fresh corn for topping

Line a non-porous dish with baking paper, allowing enough paper to fold back over the fish to seal. Combine salt, sugar, beetroot, juniper berries and lemon and place half the mix in the base of the dish. Place fish on top and then remaining mix, cover with paper and place in the fridge. After 18–24 hours remove fish from the fridge and turn over in the mix.

Return to the fridge for another 12–18 hours. The fish will be firm but not leathery when cured. Remove from mix and rinse. Dry and slice very thinly.

Preheat oven to 170°C. Combine all cornbread ingredients. Place in a prepared loaf tin and smooth top with the back of a spoon. Press some fresh whole sage leaves on to the top of the batter and sprinkle over some extra fresh corn. Bake for 30–40 minutes or until it springs back when gently pressed and cooked through.

Allow to cool before slicing.

Saltbar Beachbar and Bistro's Red Snapper and Braised Fennel

with cherry tomato, kalamata olive and caper salsa and pesto oil

SERVES 2

2 x 200gm pieces red snapper, skin on
1 large bulb fennel
1 punnet cherry tomatoes
75g Kalamata olives, pitted
75g washed capers
100g pesto oil
2 stems flat-leaf parsley
1 cup chicken stock
2 tbs of butter
2 sprigs fresh thyme
1 cup white wine
seasoning

To make the salsa, combine cherry tomatoes sliced in half, olives, capers, chopped parsley and seasoning in a bowl. Add a small amount of pesto oil and mix thoroughly. Set aside in the fridge.

For fennel, cut into wedges. Place in an oven-proof dish with chicken stock, butter, thyme, wine and seasoning. Cover with baking paper, seal with foil and place in a hot oven to braise for 25-35 minutes depending on size.

Add a little oil to a hot pan, place the seasoned snapper skin-side down and cook for 3 minutes. Turn over and cook for a further 3 minutes then finish cooking in the oven until flesh is white through the centre of the fillet.

To serve, place fennel on a plate. Place snapper on top of fennel, add a couple of spoonfuls of salsa next to the snapper, garnish with rocket and drizzle with pesto oil.

Seared Scallop and Pumpernickel Canape

by Saltbar Beachbar and Bistro

MAKES 6

6 scallops, roe on
pumpernickel cocktail rounds
salmon roe (red or black)
lemon-infused olive oil
micro herbs

Season scallops with salt and black pepper, then seal in a hot pan, 1 minute each side, in a little oil. When cool, remove roe and slice very finely.

To assemble canapés, place 1 scallop on top of a pumpernickel round. Arrange finely sliced roe on top of scallop and garnish with salmon roe and micro herbs. Drizzle a small amount of lemon-infused olive oil over the top.

saltbar.com.au saltvillage.com.au

Beetroot Relish

by Saltbean Espresso Bar

SERVES 6

250ml cider vinegar
5 tbs brown sugar
1 tsp ground cloves
½ tsp ground yellow mustard seeds
800g beetroot, scrubbed and coarsely grated
2 granny smith apples, coarsely grated
juice of 1 orange

Combine vinegar, orange juice, sugar, cloves, mustard seeds and 2 teaspoons of sea salt in a saucepan over medium heat and bring to the boil. Add beetroot and apple and cook, stirring occasionally, until just tender.

saltvillage.com.au/salt-bean

Mahsuri's Slow-Cooked Sweet Bangalow Pork Shoulder

with Cudgen sweet potatoes and parsnips

SERVES 6

1kg pork shoulder, cubed
2 tbs minced garlic
8 fresh bay leaves
1 cup chicken stock
1 cup white vinegar
1 cup light soy sauce
2 tbs whole black peppercorns
cooked potatoes and root vegetables of your choice
rice
chopped chillies

A day before combine the pork, soy and garlic and marinate overnight.

In a large heavy pot introduce all remaining ingredients, bring to the boil and then turn down the heat and slowly simmer for at least 90 minutes or until tender.

Before serving introduce cooked potatoes or root vegetables of your choice, serve with rice and freshly chopped chillies.

Steven Snow's Tian of Tuna Sashimi

with tobiko, shiso cress and miso mayonnaise

SERVES 6

6 pieces sashimi-grade tuna fillet
3 avocados
white fish fillet such as blue eye or snapper
rice flour
anchovy fillets

Yakumi mix
5g ginger
5g garlic
25g red onion
5g green shallot (spring onions)
5g basil

Miso base
100g saikyo miso
25ml mirin
25ml sake
10g Japanese sugar

Miso mayo
120g mayo
110g miso base
1 tsp Japanese rice vinegar
1 tsp dijon mustard

Soy Agar sauce
120ml Kikkoman soy sauce
120ml sake
60ml mirin
1 tsp agar powder

For yakumi mix, peel and chop all ingredients extremely finely. Wrap them in a cloth and wash under the tap to remove impurities. Squeeze out water.

For miso base, place the mirin, sake, miso and sugar in a pot. Bring to the boil then simmer for 30 minutes, stirring regularly. Remove from heat.

For miso mayo, mix all the ingredients together in a bowl. Adjust consistency with a little water if necessary.

For soy agar sauce, place all ingredients in a pot and whisk to dissolve the agar. Bring to the boil and simmer for 5 minutes. Pour into a tray and allow to set like a jelly. Once set, place the jelly in the Robot Coup and blitz to form a jelly sauce. Pour into a squeeze bottle for serving.

For fish chips, finely slice fish fillet such as snapper or blue eye into thin sashimi slices. Dust the slices in rice flour then place between two sheets of baking paper, sprinkling the slices with finely chopped anchovies. Bash the fish with a rolling pin or meat mallet until about 2mm thick. Deep-fry at 160°C until golden and crunchy and the bubbles stop. Allow the chips to cool on paper towel and store in an airtight container for up to 2 days.

To assemble, place 3 tablespoon diced tuna in a bowl. Add 1 tablespoon diced avocado, 1 teaspoon soy agar sauce and 2 teaspoon of yakumi mix. Stir to combine.

Use a 9cm ring cutter to make a tian (layered dish) of tuna-mix on the plate. Cover the tian with a layer of black tobiko then remove the ring. Scatter a little orange tobiko over the black tobiko and garnish with red and green shiso cress. Place a 'comet' of miso mayo at the top of the plate. Place 5 dots of soy agar sauce in descending size at the bottom of the plate.

Place a small amount of wasabi in the middle of each dot. Place 3 fish chips in a glass ramekin to the right of the plate.

Sea Salt Ristorante

Yamba King Prawn Risotto

SERVES 1

100g arborio rice
300ml chicken stock, boiling
4 Yamba king prawns, peeled and deveined
50g chorizo
20g pistachio nuts, roasted
4 cherry tomatoes, halved
1 clove garlic
20g onion, chopped
50ml fresh tomato sauce
salt and pepper
20g butter
20ml olive oil
basil or parsley

Sauté onion, garlic, chorizo and rice in olive oil until translucent then gradually add chicken stock. Stir continuously until rice is soft and creamy. When stock is almost absorbed add tomato sauce, pistachio nuts, cherry tomatoes, butter and season to taste with salt and pepper.

Grill or pan fry prawns separately and season to taste.

To serve, spoon cooked risotto on to plate, top with prawns and garnish with parley or basil.

seasaltristorante.com saltvillage.com.au

Bellini's

Flaming Haloumi

SERVES 2

1 x 250g block of haloumi
flour
good quality dried oregano
sumac
sea salt
pepper
Grappa

Salad

4 cherry tomatoes, halved
¼ Spanish onion, thinly sliced
3 or 4 artichoke hearts, sliced
handful of black olives
fresh basil, to taste
extra virgin olive oil or vinaigrette of your choice

To serve

lemon wedges dipped in sumac, to serve
char-grilled ciabatta bread, to serve

Slice the haloumi in half and coat lightly with flour on both sides. Place down on to the barbeque hot-plate or a cast-iron pan on the stove top, season top side with a pinch of salt and pepper and sear for 2 minutes.

Turn haloumi over, sprinkle with sumac and oregano and sear until soft, approximately 1 minute. Pour 5ml of Grappa over haloumi at the last minute before removing from the hot plate or cast-iron pan and serve while still sizzling.

To make the accompanying salad, mix all ingredients in a bowl and dress with either extra virgin olive oil and balsamic vinegar or vinaigrette of your choice.

Serve with lemon wedges and ciabatta.

*If serving on cast-iron plate, preheat plate in oven for 5-10 minutes.

Piccolo Gelato Passionfruit Sorbet

SERVES 30

700g caster sugar
500g fresh passionfruit
1½ ltr water

In a saucepan dissolve sugar in water, bringing to the boil and allowing to simmer.

Halve passionfruit and add pulp to sugar syrup and simmer for several minutes. Strain into container and freeze.

facebook.com/PiccoloGelatoaus saltvillage.com.au

Spice Den's

Duck pancakes

SERVES 1

Asian Peking duck pancake pastry packet
coriander leaves
sliced cucumber
broken up lychees (if not in season tin is ok but not preferable)
finely sliced red onion
Thai basil leaves
dried shallots

Chilli vinegar dressing

1 long red chilli – finely chopped
1/3 cup rice vinegar
pinch of white sugar
stirfried duck meat
50g cooked duck meat per person, I like to roast a whole duck and then pick the meat off of it into strips
1 tbs crushed garlic
1 tbs finely chopped coriander root
1 tbs finely chopped ginger
100ml soy sauce
100ml hoisin
50ml chinese cooking wine (shao xing)
50ml vegetable oil

Soy dressing

100ml sweet soy sauce
150ml rice vinegar
1 knob ginger, smashed
1 birds eye chilli, smashed

Stir to combine the chilli vinegar dressing ingredients.

Put oil in pan and heat, add garlic, ginger and coriander root, stir until starting to soften, then add duck meat. Stir in soy, hoisin and shao xing until combined and hot. Turn off and keep warm.

Bring to boil, then take of heat. Cool the mixture and leave to infuse.

Prepare the pancakes.

To assemble the pancakes, I generally warm the pancake first in a pan (or in the microwave is fine). I will then put on about 30-50g of the warmed duck meat, and drizzle over some of the soy dressing. Then you can garnish with all other salads and herbs and finish by topping with just a touch of the chilli vinegar mix and dried shallots. Add as much or as little of the salads, herbs and garnish as you like.

I also like to place the pancakes out not made up and let everyone make their own according to their taste.

Osteria's

Lia's goats cheese soufflé

SERVES 4-6

40g melted butter (and extra for brushing moulds)
40g plain flour
1 cup of milk, warmed
60g soft goat's cheese
20g finely grated parmesan cheese
1 tbs chopped chives
1 tbs chopped parsley
3 eggs, separated
1 egg white

Cheese sauce

1 tbs olive oil
2 cloves garlic
2 cups pouring cream
80g goats cheese
1 tbs finely grated parmesan

Melt extra butter, brush mould with butter and then place in fridge to solidify. Repeat so that you have 2 layers of cold butter on moulds before adding soufflé mix.

To make soufflé mix, melt butter in saucepan, add flour, stir over medium heat until lightly brown.

Gradually stir in warm milk, stirring continuously until mixture comes to a boil and thickens (may need a whisk to get lumps out). Remove from heat and stir in herbs and cheeses. Season to taste. Add yolks 1 at a time, beating well after each.

In a separate clean bowl. Whisk egg whites with a pinch of salt until stiff peaks form (best to use a electric beater for this).

Softly fold the egg white and base soufflé mix together. Pour or spoon the soufflé mixture 2/3 full in each mould. Place moulds in a water bath of hot water filled half way up the outside of the moulds.

Put in oven at 180°C for 12 minutes or until puffed and golden. Let cool slightly in water bath and then pull out of water and let them cool to room temperature before turning them out upside down onto tray lined with baking paper.

Cover and place the souffles in the fridge to keep until you are ready to reheat and serve.

To cook the cheese sauce, saute the garlic in the olive oil on a low heat, being careful not to brown. Then add cream and the cheese and stir until it has boiled, then turn off and keep warm until serving.

To re-heat souffles, place face down on a baking paper lined tray and pop straight into a hot oven (180°C). Cook for about 10 minutes until golden on outside and warm on inside. The soufflé should re-puff during this cooking process. Serve straight away with a drizzle of the cheese sauce over the top, and a lovely side salad of fresh rocket and parmesan, or some nice baby vegetables like beetroots or asparagus.

Enjoy!

Kartel's

Coffee Cupcakes

MAKES 12 CUPCAKES

1 1/3 cup flour
1/3 cup unsweetened cocoa powder
1 tsp baking powder
½ tsp baking soda
¼ tsp salt
½ cup whole milk
½ bottle Kartels cold drip coffee or ½ cup strong brewed coffee
1½ tsp espresso powder
1 tsp vanilla extract
200g unsalted soft butter
½ cup granulated sugar

Espresso buttercream icing

200g unsalted softbutter
2½ cups icing sugar
1½ tsp vanilla extract
½ kartels cold drip coffee or a cold espresso coffee
coffee beans to decorate
½ cup light brown sugar
1 egg at room temperature

Mix the espresso powder into the brewed coffee until dissolved; set aside to cool to room temperature.

Preheat the oven to 180°C and line a standard-size muffin tin with paper liners. Whisk together the flour, cocoa powder, baking powder, baking soda and salt.

Beat the butter and both sugars together on medium-high speed until light and fluffy, about 2-3 minutes. Add the egg and beat until combined. In a measuring cup, combine the milk, brewed coffee mixture and vanilla. Slowly add the flour mixture to the butter mixture, alternating with the coffee mixture, ending with the flour mixture.

Divide the batter evenly between the 12 liners. Baking for 20-25 minutes or until a skewer inserted in the center of a cupcake comes out clean. Cool completely before frosting cupcakes. Mix the espresso and vanilla extract and set aside to cool.

Whip the butter on medium-high speed for 5 minutes, stopping once to scrape the sides of the bowl. Reduce the mixer speed to low and add the icing sugar a little at a time, waiting until it is mixed before adding more. Once all of the icing sugar has been added, scrape the sides of the bowl and increase the speed to medium-high and whip until fluffy, about a minute or two. Add the espresso and vanilla mixture and continue to mix at medium-high until it is completely incorporated, scraping the sides as necessary.

Use a piping bag to pipe the mixture on and decorate with a coffee bean.

facebook.com/pages/kartel-espresso

Ilias the Greek's

Loukoumathes

MAKES 100

500g lukewarm water
7g dry yeast
500g plain flour
20g sugar
5g salt
oil for deep-frying (I like using organic sunflower oil)
honey for topping
cinnamon for dusting
crushed toasted walnuts

Dissolve the yeast in the warm water.

Combine the flour, sugar and salt and sift them into a large mixing bowl.

Gradually add the water and beat until you have a smooth batter.

Scrape the sides of the bowl down then cover with cling-film.

Leave the batter in a warm place for 1 hour or until holes appear on the surface.

Heat the oil to 180°C.

Using one hand, squeeze the batter on to a wet teaspoon while maintaining as much air in the mix as possible, then drop the mixture into the oil.

Repeat until you have enough for the first serving.

Cook until golden then drain on absorbent paper.

Serve hot with lashings of local honey, dusted with cinnamon and topped with crushed walnuts

Note: Make sure the oil temperature remains as close to 180°C during cooking to create a crispy shell.

Chef Samantha Gowing & Nelly le Comte's

Beet, Fig and Fingerlime Salad

SERVES 4

4 figs, quartered
1 medium sized beetroot, peeled and very finely sliced
1 red plum, pitted and finely sliced
½ Spanish onion, peeled and finely sliced
½ cup fresh basil leaves, lightly torn
½ cup assorted fresh sprouts
1 tbs French beetroot fermented kraut

Vinaigrette

1 orange, juice only
75 ml raspberry vinegar
150 ml extra virgin olive oil
freshly ground black pepper

Peel and finely slice onions. Carefully slice beetroot.

Carefully place figs, beet slices, plums and onion onto 4 serving plates.

Add torn basil leaves, sprouts and French beetroot kraut.

Whisk orange juice with the raspberry vinegar, pepper and oil and drizzle vinaigrette over salad.

Cabarita Ocean Health Retreat's Seared Salmon with Ginger Ponzu Dressing

with a salad of sea vegetables, kelp and zucchini noodles

SERVES 4

4 x 150g salmon fillets, skin off
1 cup sunflower sprouts
½ cup tamari (gluten-free soy sauce)
¼ cup freshly squeezed orange juice
2 tbs freshly squeezed lemon juice
1 tsp freshly grated ginger
1 tbs filtered water
1 tbs mirin (Japanese rice wine)

Salad

3 zucchini
1 pkt kelp noodles, rinsed well and drained
1 cup spinach, washed and dried thoroughly
1 toasted nori sheet, shredded
1 tbs arame seaweed, soaked and drained
1 tbs wakame seaweed, soaked and drained
¾ cup activated almonds, roughly chopped
1 tbs pickled ginger, shredded

Salad dressing

¼ cup macadamia nut oil
2 tbs mirin
1 tbs tamari
1 tsp miso paste
1 tsp grated ginger
1 lime, zest and juice

Preheat oven to 170°C.

Line an oven tray with baking paper and place the fish on baking paper and bake for 7 minutes.

For the ponzu dressing, combine all ingredients in a small saucepan and simmer over a moderate heat for 5 minutes to reduce and slightly thicken.

Remove the sauce from the heat and drizzle over the fish.

For the salad, use a vegetable spirooli to process the zucchini into spiral noodles.

Rinse and refresh the kelp noodles, drain and set aside.

Combine the sea vegetables, leaves and almonds and gently add the soba noodles being careful not to break them up and add the pickled ginger.

Whisk the dressing ingredients together well and blend into salad.

Serve immediate with a salad of sea vegetables, kelp and zucchini noodles.

UKI
SCHOOL OF ARTS

Stokers Siding Pottery

Sample Food Festival's

Lamb Curry

SERVES 4

1kg lamb, diced
5 green cardamom pods
5 whole cloves
2 bay leaves
10 black pepper corns
½ tsp cumin seed
2 onions, finely chopped
2 tsp chopped garlic
2 tsp ginger, chopped
1 tsp coriander, ground
1 tsp cumin, ground
1 tsp tumeric
½ tsp fresh chilli
1 tsp salt
2 tomatoes, chopped
2 tbs fresh coriander, chopped
4 tbs vegetable oil

Heat oil in a large saucepan.

Add all whole spices and onion. Fry until golden brown, then add ginger and garlic. Cook for two minutes and then add diced lamb and all of the ground spices. Stir thoroughly so meat is covered in the onion spice mixture then add the tomatoes and one cup of water.

Cook for 45 minutes on a medium heat, checking every 10 minutes to avoid the mixture sticking to the pan.

Serve with white rice and fresh coriander.

Salumi Australia's

Guanciale, Scallop and Blood Sausage on Green Lentils

SERVES 1

2 slices of Salumi Australia Guanciale
scallops (roe off)
200g blood sausage, thickly sliced
½ cup green lentils
1 medium carrot, roughly chopped
1 medium onion, roughly chopped
1 medium celery stalk, roughly chopped
1 garlic clove smashed
1 small baby carrot, peeled
cold water
thyme
olive oil
seasoning to taste

Soak the green lentils for 1 hour to soften, rinse off and place in a medium saucepan with onion, carrot, celery, garlic, seasoning and cover with cold water. Bring to the boil, reduce heat and simmer for 15 minutes or until cooked.

In a moderate oven bake the baby carrot in a tray drizzled with olive oil, seasoning and fresh thyme for 20 minutes or until golden and tender.

Place a small amount of olive oil in a pan or grill on high heat. Thickly slice the blood sausage and cook for 30 seconds either side, so that an even crust forms and the sausage is heated through and the fat is slightly rendered.

In a separate pan or grill, heat a small amount of olive oil on high heat. Cook the seasoned scallop for 30 seconds either side to caramelise and heat through.

Fry off the thinly sliced Guanciale until golden.

Spoon the lentils onto a plate lightly drizzle in olive oil. Place the scallops and blood sausage side by side on the lentils. Top the scallops with golden Guanciale and garnish with the cooked baby carrot and thyme.

Black and White Catering's

Veal Scaloppine

SERVES 4

800g veal fillet or loin
1 small bunch of fresh thyme
4 tbs butter
4 tbs olive oil
1 large diced brown onion
1 cup marsala wine (Italian wine fused with herbs and spices)
20 button mushrooms
1 cup thickened cream
salt and pepper to taste
flour to dust veal

Cut veal against the grain into 12 even pieces.

Place baking paper between pieces of veal and gently flatten with a meat mallet until 1cm thick.

Heat oil and butter in a large cast iron pan until it begins to smoke.

Salt and pepper both sides of the veal and gently dust in flour.

Place in the pan and cook for two minutes either side until golden brown.

Add onion and olive oil and cook until tender, then add wine and mushrooms. Stir on low heat until cooked. Once cooked, stir in thickened cream and heat through; do not boil.

Remove from the pan and add to the plate and serve with chat potatoes and steamed vegetables.

Fat Belly Kaf's Figs

with prosciutto, Nimbin Valley Goats Feta, pecan crumble and lavender-infused honey

SERVES 6

6 large figs
100g goats milk feta or chevre
6 thin slices prosciutto
¼ cup honey
¼ tsp or 1 head of lavender (dry or fresh)
juice of 1 lemon
2 tbs good quality pecans
2 tbs natural oats
1 tbs soft butter or margarine
2 tbs plain flour
½ tsp coriander seeds, toasted and ground
½ tsp cumin seeds, toasted and ground
¼ tsp cinnamon, ground
¼ tsp nutmeg, grated

Preheat oven to 180°C.

Place honey in a heavy-based saucepan with lemon juice and lavender. Gently warm through, do not boil. Remove and allow to infuse.

Make the crumble by toasting the pecans and oats till golden brown then finely chop by hand or pulse in a food processor.

Place in a bowl and rub in butter, spices and flour with your fingertips till mixture resembles chunky breadcrumbs, adding a little more flour or oats if necessary.

Spread the mixture out on an oven tray and bake for 5 minutes or until it starts to go a little crunchy.

For the Figs, bless the tops with a cross made by cutting 1/3 of the way down each one. Take a small cube of desired cheese, about 2cm wide, and stuff into the opening.

Placing the fig base-down on a chopping board, wrap the length of thinly-sliced prosciutto around it and tuck one end under. Secure if necessary with a toothpick then place on a lightly olive-oiled baking tray. Repeat the process with the remaining figs.

Stuff approximately 1 teaspoon crumble mix into the top of the prepared figs then bake for 10 minutes. Transfer immediately to a serving plate, sprinkle with more crumble and drizzle with the infused honey.

Raw Ecstasy's

Alive Pad Thai Noodles

SERVES 2

2 tbs tamarind paste
3 tbs wheat-free tamari sauce
3 tbs honey, agave or coconut nectar
2 garlic cloves, peeled and chopped finely
1-2 bird's eye chillies, depending on your taste buds
2 tsp finely chopped lemongrass
4 tbs coconut oil (optional)
¼ tsp Celtic salt
¼ of sm Jap pumpkin (optional)
1 large daikon radish
2 carrots
2 apples
2 young coconuts, flesh removed
1 cup finely shredded red or white cabbage
1½ cups red onion, finely sliced
¼ cup fresh coriander, roughly chopped
raw chopped peanuts to garnish

The noodle sauce

To make the noodle sauce, place tamarind paste, tamari and your sweetener of choice into a metal mixing bowl. Add garlic, chillies, and lemongrass and blend with a stick blender until you have a smooth sauce. Add salt and lastly the melted coconut oil if using.

Using a potato peeler, create long ribbons of the pumpkin. Make radish, carrot and apple 'noodles' by using a spiraliser or a grater, (you can julienne them too). Slice the coconut flesh into thin strips. Into a bowl place the noodles, sauce and remaining ingredients. Gently combine together until all are evenly coated and serve in a banana flower or on a banana leaf plate.

Madura Tea's

Lemon Myrtle Crème Brulee

SERVES 4

2 tsp Madura Tea Australian Lemon Myrtle Tea – loose leaves
375ml whipping cream
125ml milk
¼ cup sugar
½ vanilla bean, scraped
4 large egg yolks
sugar for brulee topping

Preheat the oven to 160°C. Put the cream, milk. sugar, vanilla bean and tea leaves in a saucepan over medium heat. Bring just to the boil. Remove from heat and cover. Let mixture steep for 15 minutes to develop flavour. In a stainless steel bowl whisk the egg yolks. Continue to stir the yolks as you gently add the hot cream mix over the top.

Strain the custard and ladle into ramekins. Bake in a water bath (bain-marie), pouring in enough boiling water to reach halfway up each ramekin, until custard is just set.

Remove from bath. Refrigerate for at least 3 hours. For topping, sprinkle three teaspoons of sugar on top of the brulee and either caramelise with a blow-torch or place under a hot grill.

Targa

Beef Cheek Pappardelle

SERVES 4

1kg beef cheek
1 sm brown onion, finely diced
1 sm carrot, finely diced
2 pale inner stalks celery, finely diced
6 minced garlic cloves
3 fresh bay leaf
3 ripe tomatoes, skinned and de-seeded
3 tbs tomato paste
1 ltr marsala
1 ltr dry red wine
sugar and balsamic vinegar, to taste

Pappardelle

500g bakers flour
50g semolina
3 whole eggs
5 egg yolks
20ml olive oil
pinch sea salt

Soak beef cheek in wine overnight.

Strain beef, reserve wine and reduce wine by 1/3. Season and colour the beef in a hot pan. Then sauté the onions for 5 minutes over a low heat then add the garlic, celery, carrots and cook for 5 minutes until soft. Add the tomato paste, wine and stock and bring to boil.

In a shallow tray, place beef, cover with wine and stock mixture. Cook covered, in 150°C oven for 5 hours, until beef flakes easily.

To make the pappardelle combine all ingredients and eggs and mix at low speed. Add extra yolks if necessary to create a firm dough.

Knead at medium speed for 5 minutes and then cover with cling film to rest for at least 1 hour.

Roll through pasta machine to create a thin pasta sheet, roll into a cylinder and cut to 3cm width pappardelle.

Strain the liquid from the beef and reduce to a sauce consistency, then add balsamic vinegar and sugar to achieve a sweet and sour taste.

Flake the beef and mix through the sauce, seasoning to taste.

Cook pappardelle for 3 minutes in boiling salted water until al dente and immediately toss through the sauce.

Finish with gremolata (chopped parsley, garlic, orange zest).

targabyronbay.com

Iced Energy Tea

Byron Bay Tea Company

Brighten your day with this clean, balanced and lively infusion of green tea, Siberian ginseng, gotu kola and mixed berries. A perky and delightful tea to pick you up in the morning or inspire your afternoon.

Ingredients:
green tea, gotu kola, Siberian ginseng, blackcurrants, strawberries, blackberries, hibiscus, rosehips, bilberries, elderberries.

Brewing Suggestions:
Place 1 teaspoon per cup (220mls) of near-to-boiling water into a teapot or tea infuser, infuse for 4-5 minutes, strain and refrigerate until cool. Serve with ice and garnish with a strawberry.

Byron Bay Tea Company

Immunity Tea

Feeling a little stampeded by life? Revive, renew and revitalise with this unique and refreshing blend containing some native Australian ingredients, lemon myrtle and eucalyptus combined with licorice and ginger. A healthy, restorative tea for busy people who want to bolster and fortify their well-being. Enjoy any time of the day, or any time if you are feeling a little run down.

Ingredients:
Echinacea, eucalyptus, lemon myrtle, elder berries, elderflowers, rosehips, licorice, ginger.

Brewing Suggestions:
Warm up in Winter. Place 1 teaspoon per cup (220mls) of boiling water into a teapot or tea infuser, infuse for 4-5 minutes, strain and serve.

Cool down in Summer. Place 1 teaspoon per cup (220mls) of boiling water into a teapot or tea infuser, infuse for 4-5 minutes, strain and refrigerate until cool. Serve with ice and a slice of lemon.

Bun Coffee's

Coffee Granita

SERVES 4

2 cups / 500ml freshly brewed Bun Coffee Strong Espresso Organic Blend (plunger method)
½ apple, peeled, cored and finely chopped
8 coriander seeds, lightly crushed
1 tsp finely grated orange rind
1 tbs sweet coffee essence*
¼ cup / 40g Bun Coffee's Organic Rapadura Sugar*
candied orange peel to decorate

Put the coffee, apple, coriander seeds, orange rind and coffee essence in a pan and bring to the boil. Continue boiling until reduced to 1¼ cups / 300ml.

Remove the pan from the heat and stir in the rapadura sugar until it dissolves. Pour the mixture into a shallow container, leave to cool then place in the freezer for 30 minutes.

Remove from the freezer and beat with a fork to break up the ice crystals. Return to the freezer. Beat the mixture every 20 minutes with a fork until it has frozen into fine ice crystals.

To serve, spoon the Granita into small chilled glasses and decorate with candied orange peel.

To create a delicious sweet coffee essence, combine 3 tablespoons organic rapadura sugar with 3/4 cup (150ml) freshly brewed Bun Coffee and cook over low heat until sugar dissolves. Turn heat to high and cook until reduced to ¼ cup (50ml).

* Can substitute with raw sugar
** Can substitute with raw sugar

Index

Jusfrute
Jusfrute FRUIT DRINKS
MAC'S
San Remo
Cohns
for QUALITY

for the producers in our region — with love

Acknowledgements

We would like to acknowledge the traditional custodians of this land.

Our sincere thanks to: Sarah Swan, Linda Machon, Clayton Donovan, Victoria Gosford, Despina Petri, Jill Kelly and Helen Fry for your assistance.

Heath Old Wares, Montanna Retreat, Casablanca for props and location photography.

Front cover – Salumi Australia

Back cover – The Beach Café, Byron Bay

Mehera Rowan – recipe page 157

Photography by Nelly le Comte with the exception of:

Kym Burrows – photos page 6, 7, 8, 9, 11, 28, 46, 62, 86, 91, 111, 142, 159, 171, 178, 187, 200, 211, 214

Sue McLeod – photos page 80,81,86

Ben Farrand – photo page 101

John Bortolin – photo page 201

About the publishers

Remy

Remy Tancred is Sample Food Festival director and publisher with several food books and magazines to her name.

Nelly

Nelly le Comte is a new Byron Bay convert, long time photographer specialising in food and more with magazine and book credits.

Published by Tancred Holdings Pty Ltd and Nelly le Comte Photography

First published 2013.
ISBN 978-0-9923010-6-4

Publishers Remy Tancred and Nelly le Comte
Photography Nelly le Comte: www.nellylecomtephotography.com.au
Design and Illustration Kym Burrows: www.kymba.com.au
Recipe editor and proofreader: Mary Nelson